Hi5ive - Aloha Edition:

A Simple Language for Communicating with Deep Understanding

Dale Stubbart

You can find all 130+ of my books on the internet at **Stubbart.com**

Enjoy!

Note: For Licensing Information, read that page before the Table of Contents.

Books by Dale Stubbart are
Like the Flight of the Swallow
Uplifting the Heart

Engaging
Well-Written
Easy to Read
Light
Decent
Different
Humorous

Book #138

Hi5ive - Aloha Edition

A Simple Language for Communicating with Deep Understanding

Rated: G
Reading Level: 7th Grade Medium

Longest Word: Indistinguishable

Licensing and Contact Information

I have written both **Hi5ive** and **Hi5ive - Aloha Edition.** I also hold the copyrights to them.

Hi5ive is the design for an App Building Language.

The **Aloha Edition** is the design for a Communication Framework.

If you want to create your own design for either an App Building Language or a Communication Framework, I would love to hear about it. You can contact me through my website: **Stubbart.com.**

If you want to base your design on my design, please contact me. There might be some licensing issues to resolve. It depends on how closely your design follows mine.

I expect that in most cases we will be able to work through any licensing issues. It shouldn't be difficult or a burden for either of us. And, I might be able to help you with your endeavor.

If you want to implement either **Hi5ive** or **Hi5ive - Aloha Edition** into a working version, definitely contact me. I can give you some details on how I would go about doing that. **Hi5ive** will be simpler to implement.

Implementing either of them will, of course, be more complicated if you decide to create a modified version. And, the level of complication might depend on how much you modify them.

But, hey! I'm ready to take on that challenge and help you do that. So long as you are!

Finding Your Way Around in this Book

The Titles of sections in this Book are preceded by . The titles of chapters are preceded by . In print versions of this book, the Titles of sections are underlined. The Title of chapters are not.

I've used some Hawaiian words and some Hawaiian Pidgin words a little bit in this book. It is after all, **The Aloha Edition.** I explain those words, so you don't have to guess at their meaning or look them up.

I'm not a Native Hawaiian Speaker and about the only word of Hawaiian Pidgin that I'm really familiar with is *Howzit?* (For, *How's it going?*)

I relied on the Hawaiian / English Dictionary – Nā Puke Wehewehe 'Ōlelo Hawai'i[1] to help with the translation into Hawaiian. [The a is a short a, but held for just a little longer than normal. u is pronounced *oo*. The e's are pronounced like long *a's*. The capital O is a long o sound that's held for a little longer than normal. The other o is also a long o, but only pronounced for the normal length of time. The i's are pronounced like long e's. This phrase means *The Book to Explain the Language of Hawaii*].

---

[1] **Nā Puke Wehewehe 'Ōlelo Hawai'i:** https://wehewehe.org/gsdl2.85/cgi-bin/hdict.

Some English words, however, don't translate directly into Hawaiian. So, I also tried my luck with Translate.Google.com. Then, I would go back and verify with Wehewehe [Explain] as I call it.

So, I might not have gotten some things correct. However, it's more likely that there are multiple ways of saying the same thing. And, I might not have chosen the most correct one.

Sometimes, I left out some words like Ka, which means *the*. I kept the 'okina (straight apostrophe) and the kahakō (overscore). Feel free to use other words, perhaps non-Hawaiian ones, if those are easier to remember.

I included an Hawaiian Pronunciation Guide as an Appendix. Hawaiian has a couple of extra characters. These are ' and ¯ . I explain how to pronounce them in that Appendix.

I explain what to do when you can't type them or otherwise need to omit them in the *Index of Pookay, HakaPookay and HalePookay.* That's towards the end of this book.

Right before the Index of Pookay, HakaPookay and HalePookay, there's an Index of the Commands. Use that if you're looking for more information about a particular Command.

Contents and Concepts

Hi5ive - Aloha Edition

A Simple Language for
Communicating with Deep Understanding

Introduction

To keep things clear, I always refer to this newest Edition of **Hi5ive** as **Hi5ive - Aloha Edition** or the **Aloha Edition.** When, **Hi5ive** is referring to the original edition, I almost always refer to it as **Hi5ive - Original Edition** or the **Original Edition.**

When the word **Hi5ive** is not accompanied by some mention of the Edition, it usually refers to **Hi5ive** generically. Though there are a few places where it refers to the **Original Edition.** Hopefully, you'll be able to tell that from the context.

For help while navigating this book, see the Index of Aloha Edition Commands towards the end.

Welcome to the **Aloha Edition** of **Hi5ive.** [Aloha is pronounced with short a's like ah and a long o.] I wrote this book to make it easier to communicate about concepts and projects. I also wrote it to make it easier to bring our dreams to life.

The most effective way to communicate can be to use consistency and to define things the same way. This way everybody knows what we're talking about.

At the same time, this method of communicating might lack warmth. And, it might feel too constrained. Still, the **Hi5ive - Aloha Edition** A Simple Language for Communicating with Deep Understanding, can be enriched to allow for warmth, ease, and freedom.

Alternatively, we can use **Hi5ive - Aloha Edition** only for those parts of the Communication where its Language will help everyone know what we're talking about.

I started creating this Language by creating the original edition of the App Building Language **Hi5ive.** You might be asking yourself why anybody would use an App Building Language to communicate.

If used correctly, I find that some constructs found in App Building Languages can be used to quickly clarify definitions and logic. Not only can this approach help those who build Apps communicate with those who don't, it can help those who don't build Apps communicate with those who do.

When you're trying to communicate a concept, some constructs of an App Building Language can help break it down, demystify it, simplify it, illustrate it, make it easy to understand. Or, as they say in the UK, *Sorted.*

Things can also go the other way when using this approach. And, when they do, they can go wrong quickly. It only helps when this approach is used well. And, some App Building Languages are not suited for Communication. **Hi5ive** (either edition) is.

In this book, I'm transforming my App Building Language **Hi5ive – Original Edition** into **Hi5ive – Aloha Edition** which is a Language for improving Communication. The **Original Edition** can also be used as a Language for improving Communication. However, the **Aloha Edition** is more expansive. The **Aloha Edition** is easier to use for this purpose in more situations.

At the same time, both editions of **Hi5ive** can be used as App Building Languages. Well, they can be used that way once someone develops them into App Building Languages. They have only been designed at this point. Both Editions can help you understand how to write things in many different App Building Languages.

Let me bring you up to speed. **Hi5ive - Original Edition** is the World's Simplest App Building Language, IMHO. Well, it would be if more than the design of that Language existed. Still, since it's easy to understand, it can help Programmers, Analysts, and End Users communicate. **Hi5ive - Original Edition** makes it easy to capture the rules that an App Building Language follows. You can read more about that Edition in my book **Hi5ive: The Simplest Computer Language**.[2]

Ten years after writing **Hi5ive - Original Edition,** I found myself enhancing it.

This is **Edition A.** However, I am currently living in Hawaii. So, this is instead, the **Aloha Edition.**

I'm greeted more often with *Hello, Hi,* or *Howzit?* than with *Aloha*. [*Howzit?* is Hawaiian Pidgin[3] and is pronounced the way that it would be pronounced if it were an English word.]

Even though, I'm not greeted often by *Aloha,* that's the greeting that I would prefer to hear. And, besides, it's the only one of those greetings that begins with *A*.

Next, I'll explain a little more about **Hi5ive - Aloha Edition.** Then, I'll get into Communication. I'll include examples of how to do things in **Hi5ive - Aloha Edition** where examples are appropriate. Still, I'll leave a lot of info about the details of that Language until later. You can find that in the Hi5ive – Aloha Edition Reference section towards the end of this book.

---

[2] A **Computer Language** or a Computer Programming Language is the same thing as an App Building Language. I think more people will have a general understanding of what an App Building Language is.

[3] **Pidgin** is a simplified intermediary language between two cultures that don't share the same language. It's there to help people Communicate.

One Final Note: Rather than calling the Original Edition of this Language **Hi5ive,** I could have called it **HI-5IVE-0.**[4] But, that would have probably resulted in my being accused of copyright infringement.

[4] **That 0** is a Zero, for the Zero Edition.

Let's Start with An Example

Introductions to App Building Languages usually include a Hello World example.[5] [6] These examples show you how to display or print Hello World! They might also show you how to format it.

The first example was written in the 1970's. And, since then, people have been basing examples of what Programming Languages can do on that Example.

I would like a Computer to be able to do something more useful than say Hello. So, let's use a different example.

Let's say that you want to move your car out of the Garage. That's easy enough in **Hi5ive - Aloha Edition:**

```
MoveFrom Garage.Car
  To Driveway.Back-Part
  Through Gear.Reverse
End-MoveFrom
```

You can see that we said where to move the car to. You can also see that we said to put the car into reverse to move it.

We can spell things out even more.

- We can specify to open the large Garage Door first (large Garrage Door as opposed to the smaller one for people).
- We can check to see how the car is parked and then decide which gear to use.
- We can define more precisely where we want to move the Car. We can light out different steps for each turn that the car has to make. For instance, we might be moving the car

[5] **Why Hello World:** https://en.wikipedia.org/wiki/%22Hello,_World!%22_program

[6] **Hello World Examples:** https://www.helloworld.org/

out of the garage and then pulling behind another car so that it can pull into the garage where this car previously was.

- When there's more than one car in the Garage, we can further define which one we want moved.
- We can add another couple of **MoveFrom** Commands to get ourselves out to the Garage and then into the Car.

Perhaps, you want to do something more complicated, like create Full Self-Driving mode[7] or *God's Eye* as BYD[8] calls it. In that scenario, you'll have to make things a lot more precise.

In this Moving the Car example, though, let's assume that we're speaking with a Person. As soon as we're both clear on what's to be done, we don't need to go any deeper.

Still, you might be talking with your child who is just starting to learn how to drive. They're the one who will be moving your car.

If that's the case, you might want to keep explaining what is supposed to happen, ad infinitum. You might want to keep explaining until they give up in disgust and shove the keys / fob back into your ready and waiting hand.

---

[7] **Full Self Driving Mode:** Where the Car does at least part of the Driving. Abbreviated FSD and also called Autopilot. General Motors calls it Super Cruise. Ford: Blue Cruise. Toyota: Teammate. BMW: CoPilot. Etc. Etc.

[8] **BYD:** A Chinese Electric Car Company whose motto is Build Your Dreams. It surpassed Tesla in the number of Electric Vehicles sold.

Hi5ive - Original Edition: Quick Overview

Most Apps have one primary thing that they do. Apps might be Calculators, Word Processors, Spreadsheet Managers, Emails Processors, Internet Browsers, etc. That kind of tells you the primary thing that they do.

Within that primary thing, Apps usually do several things. A Calculator App adds, subtracts, multiplies and divides. It will probably calculate the square root. It might convert between miles and kilometers.

There is at least one App that does nothing.[9] In fact, I've written a few Apps that did nothing. But, that was unintentional.

Apps define things, move them around, transform them, decide what to do next, and more.

Apps are made up of Commands – action statements. These Commands let an App do its thing. **Hi5ive - Original Edition** has very few Commands. So, they're easy to remember. And, each Command follows a simple syntax that is similar to the syntax of every other Command.

Hi5ive - Aloha Edition has those Commands[10] in its Language, plus a few more. Those extra Commands are also easy to remember for the same reasons.

---

[9] **An App that does nothing.** There's an IBM Mainframe Utility Program (App) called IEFBR14. It basically does nothing. You use it to create and delete files. You can also use it to change some file attributes. IEFBR14 does this by passing information to the operating system. An operating system is the core App of a Computer.

[10] **The Aloha Edition contains the same Commands as the Original Edition** with a few minor changes. The **Aloha Edition** also contains more Commands than the **Original Edition.**

The main Commands in **Hi5ive - Original Edition** are **Define, Move, If,** and **Perform.**

Define defines things.

Move copies things. [In the **Aloha Edition**, **Move** is now **Copy.**]

If makes decisions.

Perform does things. [**Perform** performs one or more Commands and/or Routines.]

The appearance of each Command is similar to the appearance of the **Define** Command below.

Define Name
  <u>**As**</u> Object-Type=Object-Type
  <u>**Options**</u> Options
End-Define

The Command Appearance: A Command is followed by a name, a calculation, or the name of a Routine [one or more Commands], or ….

The Command ends with **End-***Command.* In this case **End-Define** signifies the end of the **Define** Command.

Each Command has up to two specifications for attributes [things to do with the Command]. In this case, those attributes start with <u>As</u> and <u>Options</u>. Attributes are also listed in the same order – <u>As</u> first, then <u>Options</u> in this case.

Note: In the **Aloha Edition,** each Command always has two attributes. However, sometimes one or more of those attributes is optional and doesn't always need to be specified. With **Define,** <u>**Options**</u> are optional.

All Commands that are created from another Command use the same Attributes as the Command that they were created from. **File** was created from **Define**. It also uses <u>**As**</u> and <u>**Options**</u>.

Hi5ive - Aloha Edition

A Simple Language for
Communicating with Deep Understanding

File File-Name
  As File-Type=File-Type
  Options Options [Optional]
End-File

Both editions of **Hi5ive** are very simple. Yet, they are designed to be robust enough to do anything.

Aloha Edition Enhancements

Enhancement #1: I changed some Commands

The form of the **Comment** Command has changed. It used to be:

Comment Comment
End-Comment

Now, it's:

Comment Comment
  Importance Importance-Level [Optional]
  FileAs Documentation-Location [Optional]
End-Comment

I added the Importance and FileAs parts to make the appearance of the **Comment** Command like the appearance of the other Commands.

Those parts also give more functionality to the **Comment** Command. More on that later.

<==>

I changed the As part of the **Define** Command. It used to be:
Define Object-Name
  As Object-Type
  Options Options
EndDefine

Now, it's:
Define Object-Name
  As Object-Type=Object-Type
  Options Options [Optional]
End-Define

--

I renamed the **Move** Command to be **Copy,** since it does copy something to something else. I added the **MoveFrom** Command for times when you want to move something without leaving the original copy in place. When you **MoveFrom** something to **Nowhere,** it is deleted.

Enhancement #2: New Commands

The next thing I did to Enhance **Hi5ive - Original Edition** and turn it into the **Aloha Edition** was to add more Commands. Those Commands are all related to Commands that already existed in the **Original Edition.** And, the same thing can be accomplished by using those original Commands. The new Commands just make it easier to see what's going on.

Using one of the Commands in ***Hi5ive - Original Edition*** *let us know that we were having pie. Using any of the new Commands in* ***Hi5ive - Aloha Edition*** *lets us now know what flavor of pie we're having.*

Our Communication might have started out with a few grunts, a whimper, a wail, a tsunami warning siren, and a giggle or two. Soon, we found out that we weren't getting our message through sometimes. We felt constricted.

Hopefully, the addition of more Commands to **Hi5ive - Aloha Edition**, helps us feel less constricted. Hopefully, they help us communicate more clearly.

Note: Commands were initially added to style websites. Then other Commands were added for other reasons. The reason that each Command was added is stated by each new Command in the Command-Specific Reference section.

Enhancement #3: ShakaBoard Help System

[*Shaka* is a way that people in Hawaii wave at each other, holding out only their thumb and little finger.

Shaka can mean *Hang Loose, It's Cool,* etc. It's an Hawaiian Pigeon word. *Shaka* is pronounced the way it would be pronounced if it were an English word.]

In **Hi5ive - Aloha Edition,** I added the concept of the **ShakaBoard.** This is like a WhiteBoard where you can look things up. Part of the **ShakaBoard** assigns an Emoji and a Color to each Command. That way, you can recognize that Command faster.

In **Hi5ive - Original Edition,** when you type a Command in **TalkStory** [keep reading], you're shown the rest of the Command syntax. In **Hi5ive - Aloha Edition,** you can also drag-and-drop that Command Template from the **ShakaBoard.**

Enhancement #4: TalkStory App / Communication Builder

[*Let's Talk Story* is Hawaiian Pidgin for *Let's Chat.*]

App Building Languages use various App Editor for building and editing / maintaining Apps. Some of these App Editors let you test parts of your App, highlight some things, get help, format what you're typing, and more.

The theoretical Communication Editor for **Hi5ive - Aloha Edition** is **TalkStory.**

TalkStory interacts with the **ShakaBoard.** You can click on a Command on the **ShakaBoard** and the Command outline will appear in **TalkStory.** You can see help that is stored in the **ShakaBoard** from within **TalkStory. TalkStory** suggests and automates the format of a Command. That includes bolding, underlining, and indenting.

Enhancement #5: Pookay, HakaPookay, and HalePookay

[Pookay is the English pronunciation of the Hawaiian word Puke which means *Book*. You can easily see why I used the phonetic spelling instead. Haka is pronounced with short *a's*. It means *Shelf*. Hale means *House,* the e is pronounced like a long *a*.]

You can use **TalkStory** to build an App using **Hi5ive - Aloha Edition.** You can also use it to build a Communication Outline. We could call those Outlines, *Stories*. But, we would confuse that with written or oral Stories. At least, I would.

The Stories that we're building are more along the lines of Books than Stories. We could call them Books, except we would run into that same confusion.

Let's, instead, use the Hawaiian word for Book. But, let's spell it the way it's pronounced: **Pookay.** [You can tell that Pookay is not a Hawaiian word because y is not a Hawaiian letter. Also oo technically always has an 'okina between the o's as in o'o, even though the 'okina is not always written. So, oo might appear in some Hawaiian words, even though technically, it's always o'o.]

You might combine several **Pookay** (books) into a Library. Apps are also combined into Libraries. Though, sometimes those Libraries are called Packages.

Really, though, most **Pookay** will be much smaller than a Library. They will be more like a Bookshelf. Bookshelf in Hawaiian is Haka kau Pookay [kau is pronounced kaoo] – shelf for placing books. We'll leave out the kau which means *for* and call them **HakaPookay.**

Library is Hale Waihone Pookay [in Waihone, ai is pronounced as long *i*. The o is pronounced as a long o.] That Hawaiian phrase means House for storing books.

Note: **HalePookay** contain **HakaPookay** and **HakaPookay** contain **Pookay.**

Also, **HakaPookay** can contain other **HakaPookay.** And, **HalePookay** can contain other **HalePookay.** You'll see an example of **HakaPookay** containing other **HakaPookay** in the Art chapter in the Exploring Complex Communication section.

Let's say that there's a particular **Pookay** in a **HakaPookay** [Book on a Bookshelf] that you want to refer to in your current **Pookay. Hi5ive - Aloha Edition** allows you to do that.[11] [Keep Reading]

Pookay are stored in Files. Pookay is a File-Type.

HakaPookay are also stored in Files. HakaPookay is also a File-Type. [HalePookay is also a File-Type.]

The following Command lets your **Pookay** know about the Music **HakaPookay** File. The sound of the shell in Hawaiian is *Ka Leo o Ka Leho*. [This is pronounced with short *a's,* and long *o's.* The e's is pronounced as a long *a's.*]

Ka means *the*. Leo means *sound*. O means *of the*. Leho means *shell*. So, this Music **HakaPookay** is called **LeoOLeho.**

```
File LeoOLeho
  As File-Type=HakaPookay
  Options Location=Location-HakaPookay
End-File
```

[11] There might also be other **Pookay** in various **HakaPookay** that someone else wrote that you can use. And, those **Pookay** might not be written in **Hi5ive - Aloha Edition.** Your **Pookay** that is written in **Hi5ive - Aloha Edition** might still be able to use them. Currently, **Hi5ive - Aloha Edition** is only designed. How it works is theoretical. So, anything's possible.

If there is a **Play** Command in **LeoOLeho,** you refer to it as **LeoOLeho.Play.**

Enhancement #6: Modifiable Pookay and HakaPookay Flow

Apps usually have a top-down flow. This means that the Commands are processed in the order that they're stated in the App. Routines can be placed anywhere in a **Pookay.** However, they are typically only performed by a **Perform** Command.

You can often control the flow of an App by breaking out of a Routine or Command like **Perform.** Most App Building Languages also provide you with the ability to jump around in the App. But, if you jump around wildly, then, your App no longer has a top-down flow.

Hi5ive - Original Edition only has a top-down flow. I didn't provide the ability to jump around.

Hi5ive - Aloha Edition, however, is for Communication. And, I jump around quite often when I communicate. So, I've added that ability through the **Start** and **Stop** Commands. See the Going Somewhere? chapter in Appendix E: Other App Building Languages.

More on Pookay and HakaPookay

In Communication, a **Pookay** would be a Reference. It might be a Reference to some methodology, a book, a quote, etc.

You don't have to reinvent or repeat the contents of this Reference in your Communication. You just have to refer to it. People can look that Reference up when they need to know more details.

Still, you might repeat some parts of that Reference in your Communication. You might especially do that when those parts help you communicate whatever it is that you're communicating.

Most of the time, **HakaPookay** and the **Pookay** that they contain, are external to what is currently being processed. And, that might be confusing because what you're processing is usually a **Pookay** or a **HakaPookay.**

Also, you can refer to the **Pookay** or **HakaPookay** that you're processing from within itself. When you do this, you treat it as though there's a copy that's external to the current **Pookay** or **HakaPookay**. [Doing that allows for recursion[12] which is beyond the scope of this book.]

You probably wouldn't do that in Communication.[13] Though, you might refer to different versions of some Communication.

There's enough in **Hi5ive - Original Edition** to handle a lot of things. The **Aloha Edition** adds even more capabilities.

---

[12] **Recursion:** https://en.wikipedia.org/wiki/Recursion Recursion is defining something in terms of itself.

[13] **Referring to a Communication from within that Communication.** I *have* been accused of speaking in circles before. That's all I'm going to say about that.

To create the **Aloha Edition,** I could have taken **Hi5ive - Original Edition** and added a **HakaPookay** called **Aloha** that would contain any additions to the **Original Edition.** But, the **Aloha Edition** was really an overhaul and much improved version.

Be that as it may, if **Aloha** had been a separate **HakaPookay,** then the format of the **Element** Command would have been:

Aloha.Element Element-Name
As Element-Type=Element-Type
Options Element-Options
End-Element

You would just stick the name of the **HakaPookay** before the name of the Command. Then, you would need to add a period to join the two. Anything that was defined in the **Aloha HakaPookay** would be usable in **Hi5ive - Original Edition.** You would just need to reference that **HakaPookay** using a **File** Command.

File Aloha
As File-Type=HakaPookay
Options Language=**Hi5ive - Original Edition,** Location=Location-HakaPookay
End-File

However, as I mentioned, **Aloha** is not a separate **HakaPookay.** It's a new Edition of **Hi5ive.** So, even though you need to specify where each referenced **HakaPookay** and **HalePookay** resides, you don't have to specify where **Aloha** resides when you're using **Hi5ive - Aloha Edition.**

Once you have created your **HakaPookay,** you place it in a Folder where you can access it later. You do this with the

MoveFrom Command, moving it from **TalkStory** to that Folder. If you want to place your **HakaPookay** with most other **HakaPookay,** you would move it to **Location-HakaPookay.**

HakaPookay often contain Routines that are frequently used by **Pookay** that you might write. Referencing those frequently used Routines from a **HakaPookay** is easier than adding the details of those Routines to each **Pookay** that you write. It will also make the **Pookay** that you write more concise and easier to maintain. It will make them consistent.

HakaPookay are also needed for advanced and complex Routines. These might or might not be used frequently. Yet, whenever they are used, they're complicated enough that you don't want to recreate them incorrectly, even if they're only used once. That might be like reinventing the wheel.

HakaPookay can also be used when you want to handle something differently from the way that **Hi5ive - Aloha Edition** handles it.

Let's say that there's a Sort Routine in **Hi5ive - Aloha Edition.** However, you've found one that you like better. Turn it into a **HakaPookay.** Perhaps, call it **Ka'ina.** [Ka'ina means sequence. ' is a glottal stop. It's like a g-sound that almost isn't there. If you can't pronounce ', don't worry about it, just omit it. At the same time, don't run the letters on each side of ' together when you pronounce that word. Say them separately. i is a long *e*.]

As with each Command in **Hi5ive - Aloha Edition,** each Command in a **HakaPookay** can also have an Emoji and a Color that are shown on the **ShakaBoard.** Those Emojis and Colors are determined by the Developer of that **HakaPookay.**

What happens when two **HakaPookay** designers choose the same Emoji and Color combination for some Command in their **HakaPookay?** That Command in one **HakaPookay** might have nothing to do with that Command in the other **HakaPookay.**

I don't see that as a problem. If it is, **Hi5ive - Aloha Edition** could specify that the **HakaPookay** Designer has to provide a logo for that **HakaPookay.** That logo would accompany the Emoji. That logo might be a backdrop / background for the Emoji. **Hi5ive - Aloha Edition** could further specify that no two logos be similar.

One of those Logos might be like this image. It contains the circular arrow of the **Perform** Command. It also has notes to indicate that what it's performing is music.

There might be a **HakaPookay** that you can use within your **Pookay** that is not written in **Hi5ive - Aloha Edition.** It will probably not have an Emoji or a Color associated with it. And, that's OK. Those are just to help our memory. They are not required, only, strongly suggested.

You might want to think of a **HakaPookay** as a Subject-Specific Help System.

Writing Pookay

Writing can be a very important form of Communication. At least it is for me. I've written over 130 books. I also write lots of documentation. Writing is much easier for me than speaking.

Each of my books starts off as a Document [File] in Microsoft Word. Microsoft Word is a Word Processing App / Word Processor. There are many other Word Processing Apps.[14]

Word Processing Apps could also be called D*ocument Content Management Apps* or *Document Apps*. They are sometimes called *Editors*. However Editors are usually simpler (have less functionality) then Word Processing Apps.

Word Processing Apps are for Written Communication. I'm going to call them *Writing Apps*. They turn words into books and other types of documents.

Key things that a Writing App does:

- Format the appearance of a document.
- Format the text (which might be considered part of formatting the appearance).
- Check the Spelling and Grammar

Of course, Microsoft Word and other Writing Apps do more than that.

Hi5ive – Aloha Edition does provide some of the functionality of a Writing App. That is done mostly through Features, Layouts, Styles, and Themes.

[14] **Word Processing App List:** https://en.wikipedia.org/wiki/List_of_word_processor_programs

Commands and Routines of a Writing App that are more advanced could be supplied by an External App. There might be a Main-App for each key function. Since each key function does a lot, there would probably also be Sub-Apps within those Main Apps. Since we're talking about Communication, those Apps would be, or would be replaced by, **Pookay**.

In **Hi5ive - Aloha Edition,** we have **TalkStory**. It already has much of the functionality of a Writing App. So, let's expand it to do more. Let's make it a complete Writing App.

To do this, **TalkStory** might need to have at least three working modes:

1) Building **Pookay**
2) Building Communications
3) Writing Reports

All three working modes would use some of the same functionality. They would also each use different functionality. And, some of the things that they did might be called the same thing. However, they might also do different things or do things differently.

Remind Me Again What We're Doing and Why We're Doing It

In this book, we're using a simple Language to enhance Communication to build simple Communication Flows. This Language, **Hi5ive - Aloha Edition,** will help you:

- Explain complex topics.
- Explain things to others who might not share your lingo.
- Set rules for how you want to communicate. For instance, you might want to gear your Communication towards a particular audience. You might want to modify it to use particular types of words.
- Develop an idea.
- Explore a concept, a dream, some deep topic.

You might be asking yourself, *Why do we need a Language to enhance Communication?* Good question.

When you just want to talk, or *talk story* as they say here, you might not need such a Language. However, you probably still use one. It might just be a list of starter questions that's in your subconscious.

That list might contain prompts like, *How's the family? Do you have any kids / grandkids? Are you enjoying this wonderful weather? Do you have any hobbies? Is that a picture of your family?*

That list might contain prompts that are more like questions that you would ask if you were interviewing someone. *Do you have any hobbies? Where do your deep interests lie? Tell me about the last time when you were mesmerized by beauty and wonder.* Or, whatever your interview questions are.

Hi5ive - Aloha Edition

A Simple Language for
Communicating with Deep Understanding

Hi5ive - Aloha Edition is an enhancement of the **Original Edition** which is an App Building Language. Upon reading this, you might want to ask, *And, why are we using an App Building Language as a Language to help us communicate?*

#1: Both editions of **Hi5ive** have a limited number of Commands / Verbs / Action Statements. That makes those Languages easy to remember.
#2: Both are complete and flexible. They can both do anything. Yet, they are laid out in a way that keep things clear.
#3: Both editions are easy to understand. [**Hi5ive - Aloha Edition** is easier to use.]

And, that's what's needed for a A Simple Language for Communicating with Deep Understanding.

Often, when we want to talk about something deeply, explore it further, turn our idea into an invention, we begin with a loosely formed Language, like English. And, that approach often makes what we're talking about less clear and sometimes ambiguous.

Using that approach makes it harder to make certain that everybody is on the same page. That's why I'm starting with something that's much clearer and more simple.

Once you understand **Hi5ive - Aloha Edition,** you might decide that you need a different Language for Communication. Feel free to create your own.

If you create your own Language, you might want to start with this one. **Hi5ive - Aloha Edition** can help you figure out how to make your Language both complete and consistent.

Hi5ive - Aloha Edition is a pliable Language. You can begin with it and rename every Command. You can add to it. If you do that, please contact me. I'm interested in finding out more about what you're trying to do.

Hi5ive - Aloha Edition lets you refer to some well known concept. It treats this concept as a **HakaPookay.**

When you find that a particular part of that concept is not quite clear, you can create your own version of that concept which is clearer. Or, you can simply create your own version of that part of that concept and make *it* clearer.

Communication

The single biggest problem with Communication is the illusion that it has taken place. – George Bernard Shaw

Communication problems can occur when speaking the same language. They can become more pronounced when various parties speak different languages.

In addition to the concepts of One-Language Communication and Multi-Language Communication, there's Multi-Point-of-View Communication. And, there's Left-Brained Communication and Right-Brained Communication.

Are we doing something, being something, or are we thinking something? Most spoken languages tend to be built around one of those three concepts.

Hi5ive - Original Edition is an action-oriented Language. That is, the end-result is action-oriented – do something, solve something. While that is true, only three of the ten Commands are action oriented. The rest are Definitions / Descriptions. This is also true for **Hi5ive - Aloha Edition** where there are about three times as many Commands. There, 9 of those Commands are action oriented (**If, Copy** and Commands like **Copy, Perform** and Commands like **Perform**).

Actually, both Editions of **Hi5ive** are Solution-Oriented. Using that Definition, each of those Commands is a step (or multiple steps) in that Solution.

Hi5ive - Aloha Edition can be transformed to fit any type of Communication. It might not be easy to see how to transform it. Let me know if you would like my help.

Both Editions of **Hi5ive** are written in English which is an action oriented language. If, for example, either of those Editions is translated into an Idea Oriented Language, then, hopefully, it becomes idea oriented, instead.

It can be useful to look at things from different perspectives – Right-Brained, rather than Left-Brained.[15] [Among other things, Left-Brained tends to be more rigid. Right-Brained tends to be more flexible.]

However, looking at things from different perspectives is not easy to do. That becomes easier when you have a tool to help you, such as **Hi5ive – Aloha Edition.**

---

[15] **Left- / Right-Brained:** See my Book – In Search of a Right-Brained Computer.

Inter-Communication

Inter-Communication can be simply two-way Communication. **Hi5ive - Original Edition** is a language which attempts to achieve Communication between two or more people. Those people see what they're communicating about from different points of view (POV). A better term for this might be Multi-POV-Communication.

Each group of people in a Multi-POV-Communication has their own language for describing what's happening. One way to help everyone in that Communication understand what's being communicated is to use a common Language that everyone can easily understand. This is especially useful when these groups of people are working on the same project, trying to achieve the same goals.

But which language should they use? English? Mandarin? There are other commonly spoken languages. Those two, however, are the only ones with more than a billion speakers.

It's easy for two people to talk about the same thing in English and think they're communicating. However, their take-aways are different, perhaps completely opposite of each other. [I don't know whether this happens in Mandarin or not.]

One reason this happens is that there are so many ways of saying the same thing. Also, totally different things can be expressed by saying the same thing.

Perhaps the best way to start solving this problem is to reduce a Language to its core components. **Hi5ive - Original Edition** does this by taking most App Building Languages and reducing all of their Commands to 10 Commands.

All 10 Commands have a similar appearance. So, you can easily remember what each Command does.

Hi5ive - Aloha Edition

A Simple Language for
Communicating with Deep Understanding

Having a limited number of Commands that look fairly similar, but yet unique, make this App Building Language easy to understand.

Hi5ive - Original Edition makes it easy for those who know how to build Apps and those who don't, to understand the logic of what an App will do. They can agree on the logic.

Hi5ive - Aloha Edition is a Language for assisting Communication, rather than an App Building Language. It has three times as many Commands as the **Original Edition.** Still, they all look similar. And, they're easy to remember.

Hi5ive - Original Edition broke several languages down to reveal their core components. The **Aloha Edition** made the **Original Edition** more usable, yet kept it simple. This allowed that Language to be geared more for Communication. As such, it can dig deeper into various topics.

Hi5ive - Aloha Edition can help you answer questions like:

- What are we really talking about?
- How exactly would we go about doing that?
- Are we doing this correctly?
- Do we really understand each other?

Left-Brained / Right-Brained

Hi5ive - Original Edition was built as a Left-Brained App Building Language. The **Aloha Edition** added some Right-Brained Features.

For some, though, **Hi5ive - Aloha Edition** is still too Left-Brained to be used as a Right-Brained Language. That notwithstanding, I thought that it was advantageous to leave some of those Left-Brained aspects in this new Edition.

The Right-Brained Features that I added to **Hi5ive - Aloha Edition** included Emojis and Colors. I added some Commands for designing what screens and websites will look like. I also expanded the Language so that it wasn't so rigid.

I expanded the number of Commands in **Hi5ive - Aloha Edition.** Yet, I kept the number of Commands at a minimum. And, that limitation is a Left-Brained thing.

In spite of that, many App Building Languages have lots of commands and lots of ways to accomplish the same thing. And, that doesn't make them any less Left-Brained. Often, it makes them more so.

Hi5ive - Aloha Edition takes Left- / Right-Brained Communication further. It seeks to allow Multi-POV-Communication on various subjects.

Left-Brained activities that could allow for Multi-POV-Communication like that come to mind: Analysis, Reports, Accounting, Construction, Statistics / Polling, 3D Printing, Strategies, etc.

Some things can have both Left- and Right-Brained aspects. Architecture can be Left-Brained. There's a lot of math involved. Nevertheless, it often has an artistic or Right-Brained aspect to it.

Hi5ive - Aloha Edition can also be used to communicate about Right-Brained activities – Art, Music, Joy, Comedy, Stories, Aesthetics / Beauty, Love, etc.

Using a language with a limited number of Commands to communicate about something which is hard to define can be challenging. Commands in any Edition of **Hi5ive** are perhaps not best suited to Right-Brained Communication.

That's OK. **Hi5ive - Aloha Edition** allows you to define your own Commands for that. You can even create Routines (composed of Commands) for that purpose.

Then, you can create **Pookay** (composed of Routines and possibly stand-alone Commands). Finally, you can create **HakaPookay** (Composed of Stories and possibly stand-alone Commands and/or Routines). Those can also be used to handle Right-Brained Communication.

Turning Commands Into Thoughts Or Vice-Versa

Sometimes, whether you're pursuing Communication about Left- or Right-Brained activities, or perhaps activities that are both, you're trying to build an Idea.

Sometimes, you're working on a project to implement that Idea. Sometimes, you're trying to get to the heart of the matter. You want to make certain that things are processed correctly.

Sometimes, you're not working towards anything. Sometimes, you just want to talk.

All talking, begins as thoughts. In **Hi5ive - Aloha Edition,** each thought is a Command.

I chose *Command* because it conveys that this thought is doing something. However, one of those Commands is **Comment,** which really doesn't do anything. It's just a note for further clarification. And, as I pointed out earlier a lot more of the Commands are Definitions. Still, I suppose that defining something can be *doing* something.

Communication doesn't have to involve doing anything. And, it often doesn't when you're talking just to talk. So, perhaps *Thought* would be better a better term than *Command.* Thoughts can become an Idea.

Defining a Language to help you Communicate

All Communication needs a Language. It works better when this Language is agreed upon by all of the participants.

Language can be a very broad term. If you and the other party don't speak the same Language, you may end up using a mish-mash of both. You might rely on your phones to translate for you.

We tend to think that Languages are made up of words. More broadly speaking, they are made up of chunks. Sometimes those chunks are more than one word. Perhaps, some of them are a phrase or an entire sentence or two. With non-verbal Communication and thoughts, those chunks can be pictures, gestures, thoughts, etc. Sometimes Communication is sent in packets which are de-chunked and broken down later.

I have provided you with the complete syntax of the **Hi5ive - Aloha Edition** Language in this book. See the Hi5ive – Aloha Edition Reference and Command-Specific Reference sections towards the end.

Hi5ive - Aloha Edition is a complete Language that you can use to communicate about anything. The base of that Language doesn't contain very many Commands. You can add Commands as you need to. But, I encourage you to keep the total number of Commands small. Routines often work as well as Commands.

Hi5ive - Aloha Edition is based on App Building Languages. So, even though this Language is simple, it might not flow right off the edge of your tongue.

That's OK. **Hi5ive - Aloha Edition** is only a model of a Language for Communicating with Deep Understanding.

You can create your own. One way to create that model is to take **Hi5ive - Aloha Edition** as your starting point. You can then, replace its words with ones that you are more familiar with.

If you create your own Language for Communicating with Deep Understanding, let me know. I might be able to help.

As you define your Language, I suggest that you use words and phrases which are familiar, simple, and clear. You might think that a certain word or phrase is clear to everybody. Still, you should get agreement on them from those who are going to use your Language.

It will be helpful to write down every word and phrase that you are going to use. Then, you can write down what each one of those words means. [You can begin with the important words and phrases and leave the rest until you get around to it. But, who's to say which ones are important. That's one reason that I think you should start your Language off small.]

Documenting these definitions will help when something is not clear. Then, you can look back at your definitions and remind everybody what is meant by them. At that point, you might have to enhance or alter your definitions and possibly your Language.

Noting and agreeing on what things mean is also helpful for clarifying your Communication Language. *I say Tomayto and you say Tomahto.*[16] But, are we really speaking about the same thing?

When something is not clear to everyone, one tendency is to add another word to make it clear. For instance, most people in your group might understand what an apple is. For those who don't, you might add the French word *pomme*. Next, you might be adding the Spanish word *manzana*. Soon, you might end up with several words to express the same or similar thing.

Sometimes though, adding alternative words does not make Communication clearer. Often, it's best to limit the words which

---

[16] ***I say Tomayto and you say Tomahto*** is a song by Ella Fitzgerald.

can be used. This, however, can lead to calling a wide variety of things a vehicle, even though what you're currently riding on is a bicycle and not what is commonly thought of as a Vehicle – a car, SUV, or Truck.

Communication is more Art than Precise Logic

Being precise and consistent can help us communicate better.

At the same time, being too precise and/or too consistent can render a Communication ineffective. We might miss important nuances.

So, it's important to know when and how to relax the rules and rigidity.

Languages change over time. New words are added. Archaic and lesser used words are forgotten.

In fact, Zipf's Law states that the faster a word falls out of favor, the faster it is removed from a language. Actually, it says, *Given some corpus of natural language utterances, the frequency of any word is inversely proportional to its rank in the frequency table.*

Facial expressions can convey meanings. Pictures and symbols including Emojis can also convey meanings. Punctuation can make all the difference in the world.

It is up to each group who is using a Language to determine how they are going to use it. They'll need to determine the rules and the exceptions for their group's use of that Language. Knowing why they're using that Language and what they want to accomplish by using it, will help.

Most Languages have a more formal version and a less formal version. The less formal version might be a shorthand version, though usually, it just includes slang or is all slang. Slang is usually a different way to say things.

How much shorthand do you allow in your Project's Communication? How much slang? How much common language? How much trade-talk do you use that only insider's in the industry understand? How often do you find yourself translating words and concepts so that others can understand them?

Like I said, Communication is more art than precise logic. It takes a knack and often daily use to get it correct. **Hi5ive - Aloha Edition** might help get you past the sticky bits.

Information Communication Examples

These Information Communication Examples are perhaps a bit more verbose than needed. In Communication, you sometimes only really need to discuss what's truly important – the Information.

On the other hand, the less important Communication helps to keep the Communication from becoming boring. It keeps the important stuff from becoming too much to the point. And, that might be just as important a part of Communication.

Who's to say what's important – you or someone else? Also, what's the purpose of your Communication?

Sometimes, you just need to get to the point. Still, if the Communication is boring, the other party might stop communicating. And then, you'll never get to the point.

While these examples might be verbose, they don't spell out everything. For instance **Printer** isn't defined. Most people know what a Printer is. In real-life, though, one Printer might need to be distinguished from another Printer. You can distinguish them however you need to.

Perhaps, you can just say **Printer** and rely on something or someone to tell you where whatever you were printing got printed. Maybe, it will get delivered to you no matter where it was printed. And, perhaps, you'll never need to know which Printer was used to print it.

When you do need to distinguish between Printers, you can use the **Define** Command.

```
Define Epson-Printer
  As Object-Type=Printer
End-Define
```

What happens when there's more than one Epson-Printer? Figure out a better way to distinguish them. I think that is best done by specifying the Printer's Location.

```
Define Printer-in-Dale's-Office
  As Object-Type=Printer
  Options Location=2nd Floor 3rd Door on the right
End-Define
```

In Communication, the first step is to define what you want to communicate about. The second step is to communicate it.

Actually, that's not always the way it works. Still, little Communication can be had until you do the defining. Or, if Communication happens before you've done the defining, either you just got lucky or the Communication was about something else.

In **Hi5ive - Aloha Edition,** it doesn't matter where you define what you want to communicate about. There are three places where you can define that:

- The first place is to define everything at the beginning of your App / **Pookay.** You might also define everything that's related to a Routine at the top of that Routine. In Communication, this is at the starting point: *Hi, my name is ....* It's during the first phrases.
- The second place is right before the first time you use or mention something.

- The third place is after you've used or mentioned something. But, this is confusing. So, I suggest that you don't do it this way when writing a **Pookay**. When I write stories / books, I sometimes introduce something before I've fully defined it – perhaps a character or a place or an event. I give it more definition later. That often happens in stories and can work well there. Same goes for Communication. That sometimes doesn't work so well in **Pookay.** And, if you're trying to be clear about things, this is not the way to accomplish that.

When I'm building an App or a **Pookay,** I like to define things as near to the beginning as I can. But, if I forget to do it then, my next choice is to define them right before I use them.

It also works well to define those things that are well known and are perhaps major contributors at the beginning. Minor things can be defined along the way as they become known or needed.

If you're going to maintain this App or **Pookay,** whatever you've defined needs to be easy to find. That's another reason for defining everything at the top. If a lot of things are defined, they need to be well organized in order to find them when you need to find them, even if that's years after you've defined them.

In some of my books, I place a Cast of Characters at the end. That way, people can look there when they forget who is whom. I could place that at the beginning. But, I want the readers to meet those characters as they're introduced within the story.

To do that in **Hi5ive - Aloha Edition,** you would create a Routine and place it at the end of your **Pookay.** This Routine would define everyone who is involved. It would define them using the **Person** Command. In order to refer to those people throughout your **Pookay,** you would **Perform** that Routine.

After the Definition, comes the Communication. After the Communication comes whatever comes next. This might be the next bit of Definition and Communication. Or, it might be a well-deserved break.

That's one flow. Another flow might be that the Communication comes before the Definition. Or, they might switch around from time to time. And, then, you might find yourself wondering, *Which came first?* And, *Does it matter?*

Information Reports and Charts

One of the first things that we might want to communicate about is Information.

- *How's the weather?*
- *What's the news?*
- *How's our sports team doing?*
- *How much are eggs selling for these days?*
- *Where can I find a job?*
- *Show me the Addresses of my Contacts. Etc.*

There are two basic ways to report Information. The first example below uses data-structures. The next uses templates. The last example presents the report as a chart.

Let's take, *How's the weather?* How's the weather where? Then, we need to ask if you want the forecast for the next 24 hours or for the next week. When we have that information, we can show you the weather at that locale, 1 day at a time or in a grid of 24 spaces, 1 per hour.

Reports for other questions might be designed differently.

The examples below give you an idea of what you would need to write in **Hi5ive - Aloha Edition** to report a list of addresses. I've provided these examples to give you a gist of what this would look like.

```
Copy Address-Table
  To Report-Out
End-Copy
```

Or

```
Copy Address-Table
  To Printer
  Through Report-Out
End-Copy
```

In Communication, you would start with the minimum. Then, you would keep adding steps and information until it was clear enough for all to understand.

Below are some of the definitions that I'll be using:

File Address-Table ... defines the input Table where all of the Information / Data resides. There is one record / row per person in **Address-Table.**

Structure Table-In defines the appearance of **Address-Table.**

Layout Report-Out defines the Report Layout. You could get more specific by also defining each part of **Report-Out** with things like format and length. I'll talk a little more about what's involved with formatting a Report in the Formatting Reports chapter of the Presentations, Visualizations section below.

Perform passes each record in **Address-Table** to Routine **Report-Routine.**

Routine Report-Routine is like a mini **Pookay. Report-Routine** copies the **Current-Record** of **Address-Table** to **Table-In.** I could copy each Part of **Address-Table** to each part of **Table-In** if I wanted to make this absolutely clear.

Next, **Report-Routine** checks to see if a person from **Address-Table** is **21** or older (**>=**) and that they are a first level (value=**1**) connection. If they are, their Information is copied from **Address-Table** to **Report-Out** and then to the Printer.

Here's the first Example of **Report-Routine.** It uses the following Commands from **Hi5ive - Aloha Edition**:

Routine is the Routine.

Comment is a Comment.

File Defines a File, Table, or other Storage Area for Data.

Structure Defines the fields in a File, etc.

Layout Define a Presentation Layout.

Perform Performs a Routine for as long as is needed.

Copy Copies something from one place to another.

If does something only when certain Conditions are met.

Reset initializes the Layout. In this example, the initial state is set when the Layout is defined with the **Layout** Command. Since there's nothing specific stated for values, the initial state is that all text Elements within the Structure are blank and all the numeric Elements are zero.

```
Routine Address-List-Using-Structure
  Comment Create an Address List using an output
structure
    Commands lists the commands in this Routine.
  End-Comment
  Commands
    File Address-Table
      As File-Type=Table
    End-File
   Structure Table-In
      Parts Name, Address-Line-1, Address-Line-2,
Address-Line-3, Address-Line-4, Phone, Age,
Connection-Level
   End-Structure

   Layout Report-Out
     Parts Name, Address, Phone
   End-Layout
```

```
Perform Report-Routine
  Using Address-Table, Report-Out
  Looping Address-Table Until End-of-Table
End-Perform

Routine Report-Routine
  Using Address-Table, Report-Out
  Commands
   Copy Address-Table
     To Table-In
   End-Copy
    If Table-In.Age >= 21 and Table-In.Connection-
Level = 1
    Then
      Copy Table-In.Name
        To Report-Out.Name
      End-Copy
      Copy Table-In.Address-Line-1
        To Report-Out.Address
      End-Copy
      Copy Table-In.Phone
        To Report-Out.Phone
      End-Copy
      Copy Report-Out
        To Printer
      End-Copy
      Reset Report-Out
        To State.Initial
      End-Reset
      Copy Table-In.Address-Line-2
        To Report-Out.Address
      End-Copy
      Copy Report-Out
        To Printer
      End-Copy
      Reset Report-Out
        To State.Initial
      End-Reset
      Copy Table-In.Address-Line-3
        To Report-Out.Address
      End-Copy
```

```
        Copy Report-Out
          To Printer
        End-Copy
        Reset Report-Out
          To State.Initial
        End-Reset
        Copy Table-In.Address-Line-4
          To Report-Out.Address
        End-Copy
        Copy Report-Out
          To Printer
          Through Blank-Line-After
        End-Copy
        Reset Report-Out
          To State.Initial
        End-Reset
      End-If
    End-Routine
  End-Routine
```

In this next version of **Report-Routine**, a Template is used for **Report-Out**, instead of a Layout. A Template is useful when creating letters and messages that combine the values of Elements with text.

I define the separate fields that are used to pass Information into the Template. Other than that, this version of the Routine is pretty much the same as the previous version.

```
  Routine Address-List-Using-Structure
    Comment Create an Address List using an output
template
    End-Comment
    Commands
     Define Name-for-Template
     As Object-Type=Field
     End-Define
     Define Address-for-Template
     As Object-Type=Field
     End-Define
```

```
Define Phone-for-Template
As Object-Type=Field
End-Define
File Address-Table
  As File-Type=Table
End-File
Structure Table-In
  Parts Name, Address-Line-1, Address-Line-2,
Address-Line-3, Address-Line-4, Phone, Age,
Connection-Level
End-Structure
Template Report-Out
  Parts Name $Name$ Address $Address$ Phone
$Phone$
  Constraints $Name$=Name-for-Template,
$Address$=Address-for-Template, $Phone$=Phone-for-
Template
End-Template

Perform Report-Routine
  Using Address-Table, Report-Out
  Looping Address-Table Until End-of-Table
End-Perform

Routine Report-Routine
  Using Address-Table, Report-Out
  Commands
    Copy Address-Table
      To Table-In
    End-Copy
    If Table-In.Age >= 21 and Table-In.Connection-Level
= 1
      Then
      Copy Table-In.Name
        To Name-for-Template
      End-Copy
      Copy Table-In.Address-Line-1
        To Address-for-Template
      End-Copy
      Copy Table-In.Phone
        To Phone-for-Template
```

```
    End-Copy
    Copy Report-Out
      To Printer
    End-Copy
    Reset Report-Out
      To State.Initial
    End-Reset
    Copy Table-In.Address-Line-2
      To Address-for-Template
    End-Copy
    Copy Report-Out
      To Printer
    End-Copy
    Reset Report-Out
      To State.Initial
    End-Reset
    Copy Table-In.Address-Line-3
      To Address-for-Template
    End-Copy
    Copy Report-Out
      To Printer
    End-Copy
    Reset Report-Out
      To State.Initial
    End-Reset
    Copy Table-In.Address-Line-4
      To Report-Out.Address
    End-Copy
    Copy Report-Out
      To Printer
      Through Blank-Line-After
    End-Copy
    Reset Report-Out
      To State.Initial
    End-Reset
   End-If
 End-Routine
End-Routine
```

Perhaps you want to summarize the information into a Chart or Graph. Let's summarize by **Age-Range.** If **Age-Range** is something that you would use often, you might want to save it as a Condition in **Address-Table.** That would require every update to Age to update **Age-Range.**

In this case, **Age-Range** is just going to be Age / 10. If your age ranges are more complicated, you will probably want to create Condition or Routine to handle them.

The Chart itself will be built using a Chart Routine which will use a Chart Structure. This Chart Structure is like an Array or list of values. We'll make this Chart a Pie Chart.

If you were building this Routine, you would have to define a lot more. Or, you would need to use a Routine that would take care of all those definitions and the logic that would be required to create a Chart. However, we're just trying to communicate what the Chart will look like. So, I'll skip that level of detail.

```
Routine Address-List-Chart
  Comment Create an Address List summary chart
based on age range
  End-Comment
  Commands
    File Address-Table
      As File-Type=Table
    End-File
   Structure Table-In
     Parts Name, Address-Line-1, Address-Line-2,
Address-Line-3, Address-Line-4, Phone, Age,
Connection-Level
   End-Structure
   Structure Chart-Out
     Parts Title, Chart
   End-Structure
  Perform Summarize-Routine
    Using Address-Table, Chart-Array
    Looping Address-Table Until End-of-Table
  End-Perform
  Routine Chart-Routine
```

```
    Using Address-Table, Chart-Array
    Commands
      Copy Address-Table
        To Table-In
      End-Copy
      Copy Chart-Array(Age / 10) + 1
        To Chart-Array(Age / 10)
      End-Copy
  End-Routine
  Perform Report-Routine
    Using Chart-Array, Chart-Out
  End-Perform
  Routine Report-Routine
    Using Chart-Array, Chart-Out
    Commands
        Copy Age Summary for Address-Table
          To Chart-Out.Title
        End-Copy
        Copy Pie
          To Chart-Type
        End-Copy
        Copy Chart-Array
          To Chart-Out.Chart
        End-Copy
        Copy Chart-Out
          To Printer
        End-Copy
  End-Routine
End-Routine
```

In case you're wondering how many types of charts there are, let me just say, *Several*. Here are the basic chart types: Bar, Line, Point, Pie and its subtype Doughnut [Doughnut Pie – now there's a thought], Hierarchy (Organization, Pyramid, …), Flowcharts, and Maps.

These types sometimes go by different names. There are advanced forms and variations of these charts. And, there are Combination Charts which combine various types of Charts into one.

For an example of Advanced Charts, think about Picture Charts. One type of Picture Chart is Map Chart. Map Charts use a map to show information. Perhaps it's a map of the World and the Countries are color-coded to indicate how they rank on something.

Other Picture Charts might use some picture other than a map. There are also charts where the data is turned into a line drawing of something. And, there are those where the background behind the chart is a picture.

An example of Combination Charts is charts which combine lines and points onto a single chart. This is in contrast to a Line Chart and/or a Point Chart.

I'll cover Organization Charts, which are a form of Hierarchical Charts, in the Organization chapter of the Exploring Advanced Communication section below.

We can make Reports and especially Charts simpler by providing an App / **Pookay** that has separate large Routines for creating various types of Reports and Charts. I'll talk about that more later.

Details, Details, Details

You're probably saying to yourself that I went into more detail than necessary with those previous examples. Perhaps I did. But, who's to say how much detail is necessary?

Certainly, if some details are not necessary, you are welcome to leave them out. I would suggest that you keep as much detail as is needed to keep things clear.

Most people will be tempted to leave **End-Copy** off of **Copy**. That's ok. Still, it ruins the consistency of Hi5ive – Aloha Edition.

Some will be tempted to leave **End-If** off of **If.** In my opinion, that will make things less clear than they should be. So, I would suggest keeping **End-If**.

I would suggest that you keep each and every **End-....** You're Communication will be clearer. And, it doesn't take that long to write / type.

So, what details do you need to keep? And, who gets to decide that?

Let's begin with the *who*. Ultimately, anyone who needs to understand something about a Communication, needs to have a say in what details are kept and at what level they're kept. Those people include implementors of any inventions that are created from the ideas that we're communicating about. They would also include important decision makers. Anyone who will be affected should also be involved.

At this rate, you might end up including everyone or almost everyone. Still, in most situations, it seems that we can't let everyone decide.

Perhaps, you'll divide *everyone who's concerned* into prioritized groups. Then, those groups, at least the highest priority ones, will give you feedback. And, you'll make the final decisions about how you'll communicate.

I could decide how I write my books. I could let a publisher decide. But, what works best is letting my books decide how I write themselves.

Still, I have guidelines. And, if a book crosses over those guidelines, I either have to adjust my guidelines or tell the book to go and find itself a different Author.

I haven't had to tell a book that yet. I'm keeping my fingers crossed.

Now, for the *what.*

- We need to communicate enough details so that what we want to achieve is what we actually achieve, or close enough.
- We want the implementors to not make mistakes along the way that are based on misunderstandings.
- We need to clearly define the beginning and end of the process.
- Likewise, we need to define key points along the way. These might be branches or loops or external processes. External processes are usually defined at a higher level than those things that are under our control.

In the previous examples, we had input and output. Those need to be clearly defined. However, in the case of the Chart Example above, that Definition might be, *Make it a pretty pie chart.*

Pie Chart is not a detailed Definition. Still, most people know what we mean.

Pretty, on the other hand, is nebulous at best. Still, those who will receive the Pie Chart, might want to leave the exact details of how it looks vague. They might want to leave the interpretation of *Pretty* up to the implementors. They might want to be pleasantly surprised.

Those who will receive the Pie Chart, might not know exactly what they want it to look like. They might want to keep their ability to make suggestions on whatever the implementors present. They might want to make changes at that point and still have the final say on the final result. On the other hand, they might want to draw a picture and say, *Make it look like this.*

In addition to input and output, you will want to define transformations that happen along the way, especially if they're not very obvious. The more complex the transformation, the greater the level of detail will be that you will want to use.

You will also want to define the parts of the input that end up in the output. In one of the examples, the input was limited to people who are 21 or older. There might be other criteria which define whether a transformation happens or not.

As long as you get those points across – key events, input, output, and transformations; you'll probably be fine.

Of course, you might be communicating something other than how to process data.

You might be trying to communicate how people can get along better with each other.

You might be trying to solve world hunger.

Or, perhaps, you're trying to create a better recipe for a mineral foot bath.

When I took Geometry, we had to specify every step when we solved a problem. After a few weeks of that, the Teacher said that we could leave out any steps that were obvious. And, I did.

Then, the Teacher asked me to tell him all of the steps that I had left out in front of the entire class. And, I did.

So, he said, *Well, you need to write down more than just the beginning and ending steps*. For most answers I wrote down five steps. For some, I wrote down a few more.

Sometimes, I want to see fewer details. Sometimes, I want to see more. I'm rarely satisfied with the amount of detail that I'm shown. That's usually because I wasn't ever asked how much detail I wanted to see.

In a perfect World, I would be shown summary information. I would also be given an easy way to dig deeper and deeper into that information.

Rather than jumping right in and trying to communicate about something, you might want to try this approach:

1st) Define that something. Define it at a high-level only. Defer any questions for now.

2nd) Define what you will need to define. You might discover other things that need to be defined along the way. But, start with what you know.

3rd) Define various parts of this something. These parts should be *manageable*. If they're not, they should be separated into more parts. You probably do not know what each and every part is at this point. So, just define what you can as best as you can, now. More will emerge later.

4th) Define the Language that you will use to define how to get to your desired result. Perhaps, this should be the first step.

5th) Define each part in detail.

Fancy that! I ended up at 5, just like in Hi5ive.

Information Screens & Websites

The difficulty of designing how information will be displayed on a screen can vary from simple to complex. If you're designing for only one size of screen, it's easier to keep things simple. Multiple sizes of screens can quickly create complexity.

How much information can you put on one screen without making it looked over-packed? What do you do with the extra information when that screen is full or when it becomes full because that screen is now a smaller size?

Often, there are action buttons or their counterparts on a screen. What happens when you press one of those buttons?

Typically, any new or changed information is verified. Then, if everything checks out, a new screen is displayed.

If some input needs to be fixed before moving on to another screen, those errors are highlighted and you have to fix them before you can move on. There are exceptions to this. Sometimes, the errors are highlighted and you can move on without fixing them. Sometimes, you don't find out until later that there were errors.

If you're looking at a website on your phone, sometimes most of the buttons are hidden until you click a button that displays them. Sometimes a phone displays things at a smaller font size. Both of these actions try to save room so that you can see more on one screen of your phone.

When I self-publish my e-books, the Page Header and Footer information that's in the Print Book goes away. Footnotes at the bottom of a page become Endnotes at the back of the book in an e-book. The Self-Publishing App does this so that more information can fit on one page / screen of a phone.

There are basically two types of information – profile and transactional.

Profile information about a customer would be their name, address, age, contact info, etc.

Transactional information could be their various bills and payments.
It could be messages or correspondence between the company and the customer.
It's things that might repeatedly happen over time.

Profile Information is usually displayed / entered / updated / deleted using one screen per object / subject / topic. So, there might be one screen for modifying, adding, or deleting the main information about a customer.
Sometimes an object has sub-objects. When this happens, one screen is typically used for the main object and one for each sub-object. Here one sub-object might be contact information. Another might be summary information about this contact's account with your company.

Typically, several transactions of the same type are displayed on the same screen. For instance, a set of financial transactions is displayed on one screen. That information might be displayed in descending order by date (latest date first).
Communication transactions might be displayed on a separate screen. These would record significant bits from conversations that a Customer had with a Customer Service Representative.

Often, grouping information by type, sub-type, etc. helps screen designers figure out which information goes on which screen. A type might be Transactions. A sub-type might be Financial

Transactions. And, under that there might be Bills and then Bill Details.

I'm not going to give examples for screens using **Hi5ive - Aloha Edition.** They can be the same as for reports. Except, reports tend to be printed. This means that, information is copied to the printer, rather than to the screen.

There also might be logic to decide what to display on a screen and how to display it depending on the screen size. The same can be true for reports. However, the size of paper for printers is pretty standard.

Screens can use colors to display Information. Some printers can print in color, but some are still limited to black ink. Black ink is cheaper. And, one-color printers are also cheaper. So, colors might not be an option. Screens, on the other hand, almost always have the ability to display things in color.

Screens might have action buttons like Add, Change, and Delete. Reports would not have those buttons. They would not need to specify what happens when one of those buttons is clicked.

I previously mentioned that Reports can be built using Templates. The same is true for Screens. Templates are sometimes called Forms, especially when they are used for Screens.

Tracking Information Changes

Changes to Information are often made by storing before and after copies of the Information.

The Before Copy is what the data looked like before the change.

The After Copy is what the data looks like after the change.

The User and/or Routine that made the change and the date and time when each change is made are also stored with both copies. Both copies of the Information are stored in a File. A Structure is usually used for Tracking Information Changes. I often looks like this:

Information-Copy	Changed-By	Changed-On

We could also store the **Copy-Type** – was this a Before Copy or an After Copy. However, **Changed-On** can be used to tell us that. The After Copy will happen at a later time than the Before Copy.

Very old computers didn't store the time that accurately. On those, sometimes **Change-On** would be the same for both Copies. Now, time can be stored much more accurately. So, that duplication rarely happens. And, I'm going to ignore that possibility, for now.

Storing a Before and After Copy of each and every change can take a lot of space. It can also slow things down.

Only storing the After Copy can limit the amount of storage that this tracking will take. Doing that is OK, assuming that the initial information, if any, was already saved. That is, the first time this information was added, an After Copy was made.

The Before Copy for the first After Copy doesn't matter because there was nothing before that first After Copy. Now, each After Copy, except the last is also a Before Copy.

Sometimes, only important Information is tracked each time a change is made. In this instance, someone has to determine what is important. Changes to the rest of the Information might only be tracked every so often.

Sometimes, all of the Information is tracked, but only when an important change is made.

The changes are stored in Tracking Files. [These are Files that keep track of things.] These Files are often called Logs. They are only kept for so long. Then, they are either archived (moved out of the main Information area) or deleted.

Determining when a change is made, requires somehow noticing when something makes a change to the Information. This could involve several occurrences of the **If** Command.

However, typically the Before Copy is placed into one Structure and the After Copy is placed into a second Structure. Both of these Structure hold the Information in the same places. These Structures are then checked with one **If** Command to determine if any part of the Information has been changed. If it has been changed, the Structure can be copied to the Tracking File.

Perhaps though, it's an App / **Pookay** that is changing the Information. In that case, do we need to track the changes? Or, do we need to track them as much? That App / **Pookay** might be less likely to change things incorrectly than a human would. [The opposite might also be true.]

Sometimes, whether a change is tracked or not, depends on the type of information that was changed. Financial and Security Information needs to be tracked every time it is changed. Anything that affects Financial Information like rates or taxes needs to be tracked every time it is changed.

To track changes at certain intervals, we need two more Commands: **Set** and **Reset.** Intervals happen at certain times during tracking. **Hi5ive - Aloha Edition** refers to these times as states.

The Initial State is before anything happened.

The Current State is now.

The Final State is when things have ended.

You can define any other states that you need.

Set sets the State of something.

Reset resets the values of that something to what they were in some prior State.

Let's say that you're working on a project to build a car. As you get to certain points in your project, you want to save what you have done so far. Perhaps, you want to apply for some patents now. In any case, you need to document your work.

You might want to save what you've built so far. Perhaps, it's your prototype. That way, you will be able to come back to this point and start from there. You might call this Version A.

As you progress, you get to another such point. You save your work and call that Version B.

These Versions can be States. However, let's say that we start making Version C. We get so far along and realize that we have to restart with Version B. I would call what we have before we restart, the final state of Version B. I would also likely call that the initial state of Version C.

One of the examples at the beginning of this section, included an Initial-State. So, I'm going to skip creating another example for States here.

Instead, let's say that you want to take backups from time to time and label them properly. Let's say that you keep a backup of every major and minor version of your project. You also keep daily backups until you reach your next minor (or major) version.

After you take the backup for that version, you can get rid of several daily backups and create a new one. Depending on how thorough you want your backups to be, you might keep daily backups until you've gone through two or three more versions.

On most projects you don't need to be this thorough. On several of my projects, I just keep the current version up-to-date until the end of the project. Then, that version becomes my final version.

In this scenario, if I introduce errors, I can manually work my way back to an error-free version. That's because I know what I'm doing well enough to correct any errors. Or, do I?

Perhaps, I'd better rethink taking backups.

Information Security

One aspect of Security involves People and their Roles.
People are defined by the **Person** Command.
Roles are defined by the **Role** Command.
Then, the **Security** Command assigns People to those Roles.

Person Who
  Is Description [Optional]
  Attributes Attributes [Optional]
End-Person

Role Title
  Is Description [Optional]
  Attributes Attributes
End-Role

Security Role
  For Person
  Access Object-Name, Access-Type, Level [Optional]
End-Security

You might want to create a **Person-Role-Security** Routine that would contain these three commands. You could then perform that Routine rather then repeating these three Commands every time you want to set someone up with Security.

At the same time, you'll probably set up all Roles once. An Attribute might be **Availability-Mode=Global**. That would allow you to use that Role anywhere. And, if your Roles are already set up, your Routine only has to be a **Person-Security** Routine.

Security also involves Access-Types for Files / Tables and their Locations. Access-Types are specified in the <u>**Options**</u> phrase of the **File** Command as:

```
  Options Access-Type=Read-Only

File File-Name
  As File-Type=File-Type
  Options Options
End-File

Location Location-Name
  As Location-Type=Place
  Options Options
End-Location
```

There is an Encryption Routine and an accompanying Decryption Routine. For Security reasons, these Routines are probably provided in a **HakaPookay** from some Computer Security Company. Perhaps, they called that **HakaPookay Palekana.** [The a's are pronounced as short *a's*. The e is pronounced like a long *a*.] Palekana is Hawaiian for Security.

Encryption / Decryption Routines can be used on the **Copy, MoveFrom,** and **Reset** Commands. The **MoveFrom** and **Reset** Command Examples are similar to the **Copy** Example. So, I omitted examples for those Commands for now. You can find those examples in the section Command-Specific Reference, chapter Copy, Draw, MoveFrom, Reset, Set.

```
Copy Element-A
  To Element-B
  Through Palekana.Encryption-Routine
End-Copy
```

What Information do you need to keep secure? First, any Information that's not yours. This is mostly Information that belongs to your users, clients, and vendors.

You'll also want to keep some of your own Information secure while providing some level of transparency. If you're defining a project with **Hi5ive - Aloha Edition,** you might want to secure that project until it has been defined, is working, and you're making a mint off of it. Or, you might want to keep it *open source* in the hopes of enticing others to contribute to the code.

There are often government regulations covering what you need to secure. Check with those government agencies when in doubt. [17] [18] [19]

[17] **Keep HIPAA (Health) Information Secure:** https://www.hhs.gov/hipaa/index.html

[18] **NIST Cybersecurity Standards:** https://www.nist.gov/cybersecurity-and-privacy

[19] **ENISA European Security Standards:** https://www.enisa.europa.eu/topics/certification-and-standards

Information Storage

Information is stored in a File. [Databases, Tables, etc. are all Files at their most basic level. So, I'm using *File* generically.] Files are accessed from a Location. **Hi5ive - Aloha Edition** provides the **File** and **Location** Commands to help you work with Files and Locations.

To make changes to a File, Information is changed in a Structure. That Structure is then copied to the corresponding record(s) in the File.

If you're dealing with a Table, then replace the word record with *row*. Now, you're talking *App Building Lingo.*

Note: A Structure is a Group.

```
Copy 123456
  To Person-ID
End-Copy
Copy Screen.Last-Name
  To Table-Z
  Through Structure=Structure-A,
     Table-Z.Person-ID = Person-ID
End-Copy
```

The above example finds the row in **Table-Z** where **Person-ID**[20] = 123456. Then, it replaces **Last-Name** in that row with **Last-Name** on the **Screen.**

Files and File-Devices can be copied using the **Copy** Command. To move them without making a copy, use the **MoveFrom** Command. A Device can be defined using the **Group**

[20] An **ID** is an Identification Number. In this case, Person-ID

Command. If you work with a lot with Devices, you can create your own **Device** Command.

When you copy a File, you might want to compress the information in the Destination File. You might also want to compress the information in the File without copying it somewhere else.

That File is probably already somewhat compressed. Sometimes, though, you might need to compress it some more.

```
Copy File-A
  To File-A
  Through Routine=Compression-Routine
End-Copy
```

Presentations, Visualizations

So, when are we going to get to Communication? We'll start into that in the next section. I promise.

Producing a Report always seems like it should be simple. Yet, those are some of the hardest Apps I have ever written. And, Presentations can go way beyond placing text and numbers on a piece of paper, which is basically what a Report does.

- Presentations can be interactive.
- Presentations can be in the form of graphs or pictures.
- Presentations can be slideshows and/or white papers.
- Presentations might even be videos or perhaps video games.

Presentations and Visualizations were never simple. These days they can be much more complex.

Formatting Reports

Reports were previously covered in the Information Communication Examples section above. Charts were also covered there.

This chapter talks more in depth about Formatting Reports. But, I won't get too deep into formatting.

Areas of a Report

Report Opening Report Header
Report Detail
Report Footer
Report Closing

A Report can have a report opening and a report closing. Both are optional. Within those, if they exist, are the Report Header, the Report Body / Detail, and the Report Footer. Each of those is also optional.

Note: If you make all of these optional, you will not have a Report. Just sayin'.

Areas of a Page

Page Header
Page Detail
Page Footer

A Report can be divided into pages. [*Report* in this case, usually refers to the Report Detail.]

The Page Header typically appears at the top of each page. The Page Footer typically appears at the bottom of each page. However, when there is a Report Opening or a Report Header, the Page Header either appears right below that Report Opening / Report Header or not at all. [The Page Header will or will not appear at the top of the next page based on the Page Header Rules for that page.]

When there's a Report Footer or a Report Closing on a page, the Page Footer either appears right above that Report Footer / Report Closing or not at all. [The Page Footer will or will not have appeared at the top of the previous page based on the Page Footer Rules for that page.]

In between the Page Header and the Page Footer is the Page Body / Detail.

Grouping, Filtering, Sorting and Group Areas

The Report Body / Detail is often divided into groups based on some filtering / sorting criteria. There might only be one group. When there is a group / are groups, there can be group headers and group footers. Between each group header and group footer is the group body / detail.

Contents of Various Areas

The Page Header contains the title of the Report. It might also contain information about the Report, like the Company / Requestor Name. And, it might contain the page number.

The Page Footer typically contains the page number and possibly the name of whatever Company or Person prepared that Report.

Most of this information can go into either the Page Header or the Page Footer instead.

The Report Header might contain filtering information [what is to be included on this report]. The Report Header typically contains the column headers. If columns differ between groups, they are typically omitted from the Report Header and specified in each group header instead, unless there are no groups.

The Report Footer contains grand totals and other summary information.

Group headers and footers. are like Report Headers and Footers, except they are only for each group of information.

Reports Layouts

Most reports are columnar. [They present information in columns]. Often there's a label or identifying information at the beginning of each row, like the Account Number / Account ID.

Layouts have to handle data that's too long to fit in the column that's supposed to hold it. Should that column overlap another column? Should that data just be truncated, end with …, or continue onto the next line. If it continues onto the next line, for how many lines should it continue?

Layouts also have to handle the formatting of numbers. For instance, Are commas displayed? Does the negative sign go in front of or after the number? Are units of measure displayed on each line or in the column header?

We can add styling to a Layout. So, we can make the Title, column headers, and labels **bold**. We can also <u>underline</u> the column headers.

After a couple of years in Saudi Arabia, I left that job so that I could get more education. About one year after I left, I heard that the Company I had worked for bought a new printer. They bought it specifically so that they could print their reports in both English and Arabic. That is, each report was to present the data in both English and Arabic on the same page.

Of course that was twice as much printed information. So, every report had to be redesigned to figure out where to print that extra info.

Summary Information

In addition to the details of the Report, many Reports contain Summary Information. Summary Information goes in the group footer and/or Report Footer area.

Data might be summed up at various levels (for certain groups of data). The highest level is grand totals. Does the User of this report want to have the last line before a total underlined?

Averages, minimums, or maximums might be reported in addition to or rather than sums.

When Reports contain sums or totals, the data is usually sorted.

A HakaPookay for Reports

There's probably a Reports **HakaPookay** that **Hi5ive - Aloha Edition** can use. We'll call it **Ho'ike** for now. [The o in Ho'ike is pronounced as a long *o*. The ' is a glottal stop and separates the o and the i. The i is pronounced as a long *e*. The e is pronounced as a long *a*.]

Ho'ike is used to specify how the data will be sorted and summed and handles that. This Reports **HakaPookay** also contains generic Layouts for presenting the data in all of the report's various areas. It controls when and whether to display each area.

Back in the chapter Writing Pookay in the Introduction section, I mentioned that **TalkStory** would be able to write reports. And, indeed, the **Ho'ike HakaPookay** is part of the **TalkStory HalePookay.**

IBM COBOL used to have a Reports Section. I converted a lot of Report Apps to use that Reports Section. That took care of most of the hard work that was involved in producing a report.

Unfortunately, that section was later considered non-standard and was removed. Then, I had to revert all of those Apps. And, I had to convert many more Apps to work without that section.

Formatting Screens

Screens were partially covered in the Information Communication Examples section above. This chapter talks more in depth about Formatting Screens.

I previously mentioned that Reports can be built with Layouts. The same is true for Screens.

Screens are similar to Reports. However, Reports are usually taller and skinnier than Screens. So, a Report might have to be redesigned to fit onto a Screen.

When I design my websites, I have to design them so that they'll display well on any screen – laptop, phone, iPad, tablet. I also take some effort to see that they print well on printers. But, most people don't print websites to printers. So, I don't spend too much time on that.

Screens typically display a single set of related data, rather than several lines of data with sums. However, that's not always the case.

Both Screens and Reports can contain several colors. However, it's more likely that a Screen will contain more colors.

You can also add pictures and watermarks to both Reports and Screens. Reports are more likely to have watermarks. Screens are more likely to contain pictures.

Interactive Screens

Screens are not just for reporting information. They can also be input devices. And, they can sometimes respond to your input right away.

Give me a million dollars

Not on your life!

That's probably not a typical scenario for an interactive Screen. But, it could happen.

When Screens are used for Input, each field can have its own validation. There can also be validation of the entire Screen. That usually involves at least validating some field(s) in relation to other field(s).

After the data is input, what happens?
Is the data stored somewhere?
Was the requested action to delete that data?
Is a log / record kept of the before and after images of the data?
Is some other action triggered?

Dashboards and Other Summary Presentations

A Dashboard is often a small Summary Report or Screen. A Dashboard typically shows statuses and counts / sums. It often shows these graphically with gauges and/or graphs. And, you might be able to click on part of that Dashboard to see the details.

Reports typically show closely-related information. Dashboards, on the other hand, often show data that is not so closely related

Dashboards are generally used to report information to upper management or to the entire company. This information often includes things like the status of a project, the operational readiness of that project, and/or the status / health of that project. They can also show these things about a Department or the entire Company.

Dashboards might be available 24/7. Or, they might only be shown as part of a weekly / monthly / etc. Status Report, Presentation, or Executive Summary (see below).

So, you've been tasked to create an Executive Summary for the Top Level Management of your company. How do you go about doing that?

An Executive Summary often contains a description of a problem and its proposed Solution. There might be footnotes or endnotes with links to further reading. There are probably pictures and summary charts. There might be tabular [tables [rows and columns]] information, like on a spreadsheet.

You might include examples. For instance, you might report on the groups who have made the most progress on a project. Or, you might report on how all of the groups are doing on revenue.

Your Executive Summary might include Reports, Screenshots, Dashboards, etc. Yet, typically, there will also be lots of text. Sounds like Templates and Layouts might come in handy here.

Many Executive Summaries are created in a Word Processing App / Writing App. You type the text into a Document using your Writing App. Then, you pull the supporting pictures of Charts, Screens, Reports, etc. into the document.

What if, on the other hand, you could have a computer generate that Executive Summary for you? You just tell it everything that needs to be included. If it needs a graph it generates it. Same for a dashboard or report.

You can see how this could get complicated very quickly. Still, if you think about how a computer would do this at a high level, it might help you break your Executive Summary down into manageable parts.

As far as **Hi5ive - Aloha Edition** goes, we have a choice:

- We can create a Writing App.
- Or, we can let a Writing App handle all of that text.

Probably what we want is some combination.

We can create the text portion of the Executive Summary in a Writing App. We can let that App take care of italics, bold, etc. formatting. We can let that App take care of checking our spelling. We can save our work to a File.

Then, in **Hi5ive - Aloha Edition,** we can create a **HakaPookay** that will read that File. Then, it will reformat the text so that it fits nicely into the size of our Executive Summary.

That App will also let us rearrange that text as necessary. And, we can omit part of it and/or add to it.

However, reading the normal output of a Document Processing / / Writing App like that can be very complicated. It will probably be simpler to save the output in a standard format. And, then have **Hi5ive - Aloha Edition** read *that* File. That standard format is usually a pdf File.

A Writing App for **Hi5ive - Aloha Edition** might be smaller that a complete Word Processor. That App will still need to include some of that complex logic, but not all of it.

Why not incorporate a Word Processor as the main functionality of **TalkStory?** We can still use that **HakaPookay** to edit **Pookay** and **HakaPookay.** Though, we might have to switch modes to do that. Another part of **TalkStory** can be the Report, etc. Routines. Now, **TalkStory** is probably the size of a **HalePookay** and contains various **HakaPookay.**

Slideshow / Presentation / Video

You are supposed to or want to create an Executive Summary. But, how many Executives are going to read it? More than likely, you'll need to turn that Executive Summary into a Slideshow. That way, they'll be able to watch it instead.

A Slideshow doesn't necessarily need to consist of slides. It can consist of *virtual* slides instead. Each virtual slide can be a portion of that Executive Summary.

Somebody might create an App that could be used in **Hi5ive - Aloha Edition** to turn an Executive Summary into pictures, one portion at a time. You just need to specify the start and end points for each slide. If your Executive Summary is already formatted into presentation size pages, you might be able to specify that each page becomes a slide.

Once you have your Slideshow created, you are ready to present your Executive Summary to the Executives. OK, so, maybe you need to practice presenting your presentation a few times first. Still, when you're ready, you can just call up the Slideshow and pause it while you speak about each slide.

Since you now have a Slideshow, it doesn't take much to turn that into a Video.

- We have to monitor the timing of each slide.
- We will need to add in audio, some of it spoken. Perhaps, some of it music.
- We might want to fade slides in and out.
- We might want to adjust the volume in certain places. We might want to adjust the overall volume.
- We might want fancy transitions between each slide.

- We might animate some slides.

Hi5ive - Aloha Edition can handle the timing with its **Start** and **Stop** Commands. See the Perform, Start, Stop chapter in the Command-Specific Reference section below for more information on that. To do a lot of the other things that were mentioned will require more **HakaPookay.**

We can turn that Slideshow into a Video. Perhaps, this **HakaPookay** will be called **Wikiō** which means Video. [The i's in Wikiō are pronounced as long *e's*. The ō is pronounced as a long *o* that is said for a little longer than normal.]

We can make a Video interactive. After a few iterations and several enhancements, that Video might become a Video Game.

If there were a Video Game **HalePookay**, we might call it by the Hawaiian phrase for Video Game **Pā'aniWikiō.** [The ā in **Pā'ani** is pronounced as a short *a* that is said for a little longer than normal. The ' is a glottal stop that separates the ā from the a. The a is pronounced as a short a that's said for the normal length of time. The i is pronounced as a long *e*.]

I figure this is a **HalePookay** that contains the **Wikiō HakaPookay.**

Exploring Basic Communication

What is involved in Communication?

- The Sender(s) or Transmitter(s)
- The Receiver(s) or Antenna(s)
- The Delivery Method(s) and Carrier(s)
- The Message(s)
- Additional Input. Facial Gestures for example. Perhaps, Sign Language or closed captions.
- Formatting
- Interference / Blocking
- Lack of Interference / Lack of Blocking
- Facilitation / Flow
- Encryption / Encoding and Decryption / Decoding, if any
- Packing and Unpacking. In other words, Condensing and Expanding
- Reception and Understanding

There might be multiple Senders and Receivers. Some might be anonymous. Perhaps, some are innocent bystanders. Others might be spies / eavesdroppers.

There are several methods of sending and receiving a message: Email, Phone, Social Media Post, and Newsletter, for example.

The Carrier might be implied by the Delivery Method. However, I think of the Carriers as being the Companies and cables / airwaves that carry the message. In the case of a Newspaper Ad, the Company is the Newspaper Company.

The Newspaper is carried by a Newspaper Delivery person or a News Bin or a local store. It might be delivered online via the Internet. This, to me, is the Delivery Method.

There might be multiple Inputs – audio, visual, etc. Those Inputs might be working together and/or against other Inputs.

When the message is sent, it might be formatted. Then, it might be condensed. Next, it might be encoded.

On its way to the Receiver, the message might run into interference. That is, it might be partially received. Or, it might be garbled. The message might be blocked or partially blocked / filtered. Noise might be added along the way. Perhaps, it was added on purpose; perhaps, not.

When the message is received, it needs to be understood. Before it can be understood, it might need to be interpreted or translated.

The message might need to be cleaned up.

If the message was encoded, it will probably need to be decoded.

If it was condensed, it might need to be expanded.

And, the message might need to be reformatted.

All of that can get pretty complex. But, let's start with some of the basics by using some examples.

Items to Define for Communication

Hi5ive - Aloha Edition can be used to process Communication. To do that, each of those things at the top of this section needs to be defined. Those begin with the Sender and the Receiver and continue through Reception and Understanding.

The Sender and the Receiver might both be simple Definitions in **Hi5ive - Aloha Edition.** The Formatting and Condensing will probably be Routines.

Sometimes important parts of the message are not received or they are garbled. Someone or some Routine will need to try to fill in the blanks and piece that message back together. This may require contacting the sender with, *Say again?*

Some sort of status needs to be returned to the Sender. This can be a question mark or a thumbs up or whatever is pre-agreed upon. Rather than a status, a new message might be sent.

That new message can include the status. But, it doesn't have to. If no status is included, then all is assumed to be well with the reception of the previous message.

A message might be sent. But, then, it is never received. Or, perhaps, it was received. Yet, no acknowledgement of its being received was returned. When those things happen, it is common to send the message again after a certain amount of time. That amount of time usually depends more on the message and the Sender, than on the Receiver.

In real life, there's a lot of junk mail including junk e-mail. Somehow, the Sender got ahold of our contact information. And, even though we never reply, they keep contacting us. And, sometimes when we do reply and tell them to stop, they don't. This, or course, is not real Communication.

I once placed an order with a certain company. It wasn't a huge order. It wasn't even a large order. My small order didn't cost that much money. I have never ordered anything from them again.

Still, every year, they send me their catalog, even though I have moved twice since then and have not given them my forwarding address. And, when I receive their catalog it goes right into the trash.

It's only once per year, so perhaps it doesn't cost them that much. Still, it is a very, very thick catalog. Even at postal rates for media, it must cost them something to send it to me. Plus, they have to print it.

Not only do I consider this to not be real Communication. It's not a wise investment of their business dollars.

Moving on, let's consider a phone call. When the Receiver answers their phone, the conversation starts. The signal that there is a message is the ringing phone.

When either Caller hangs up, the conversation ends. That signal is the dial tone. That signal might occur when one person says, *Good-bye*. However, that person might say, *Good-bye,* multiple times before the conversation really ends.

Other messages might likewise need start and stop signals. In App Lingo this is a Start-of-Message and an End-of-Message. An End-of-Message can be triggered when neither party has spoken for a while. It can also be triggered by a crying baby.

Events, Their Initiators and Terminators

Events are things that happen. But, then, you already knew that. Events happen on a schedule. Or, at least they're supposed to. I suppose you already knew that also.

Even when Events are impromptu. They still happen at a certain place and time. But, impromptu means that they kind of happen on a schedule more or less. Sometimes, we might even be able to predict when an impromptu Event will happen. Yet, the more we're able to predict it, the less impromptu it will be.

So, let's leave random acts of kindness and other impromptu Events out of the equation for now. Let's focus instead on planned Events.

What starts an Event? Well, you might say that planning starts an Event. We'll get to planning in a bit. Let's assume for now that the Event is already planned. It's on the schedule. What starts it?

Well, a timer might start it. But, some Events are not set to happen when the clock reaches a certain time. Some Events happen when it's been so many minutes since a previous Event occurred. Again, a timer is involved. But, also a sequence or flow of Events is involved. And, when it's this Event's turn and enough of the Conditions are met, it starts.

And, there are planned Events which follow a flow, but are not set to start at a given time. Let's say that these events are on a *non-time-based schedule.*

There might be a pause before an Event starts to let other Events catch up. So, there might be a trigger involved. The trigger might say, *When a certain set of Events has occurred, this Event can start.*

Sometimes, an Event can't start until a person does something. That might be pressing a button on a computer screen. Perhaps, they have to turn on the TV. Perhaps, they have to set the alarm before they leave the house. Maybe, they just need to arrive at the store before they can start shopping. Perhaps, we're waiting on them to start this event.

Maybe it isn't a person. Maybe, it's their dog. Their dog has to indicate that now would be a good time to take it for a walk. Right now! Really!!

These things that start actions are called Initiators. The things that happen before an action can happen are called Predicates. I remember that because they predate[21] the Event. When I C [see] that those things have predated the Event, it can start. [*I* and *C* are the letters remaining when predate is removed from *predicate*.]

Scientists have now proven that there was time before the Big Bang. Not very much time, mind you. Still, some things did predate that Event.

In **Hi5ive - Aloha Edition,** Events are scheduled with the **Start** and **Stop** Commands.

```
[Start - Starts an Event.]
Start event
  Using Date-Time [Optional]
  Looping Location=Location-A, Start-
Condition=Condition-A, Stop-After=Time-A1, Start-
At=Time-A2, Stop-After=Time-B1,
Stop-At=Time-B2, Stop-Condition=Condition-B
```

[21] **Predate** might seem to imply that a previous event happened at least one day ago. Alas, that is not the case. Predate just means *before*. Perhaps, we should change that word to *Pretime*.

End-Start

[**Stop** - Stops an Event.]
Stop event
Using Date-Time [Optional]
Looping Stop-Condition=Condition-A, Stop-After=Time-A1, Stop-At=Time-A2, Stop-For=Time-A3
End-Stop

Each Event can be thought of as a transaction. Each step of an Event can also be thought of as a transaction. You can also think of events as major transactions and steps as minor transactions.

Unless things are in an endless loop, there will be one step that ends an Event. Though, the same step might not end every Event. And, a different step than normal might end the same Event, depending on circumstances.

Even if an Event does end up being in an endless loop, eventually, something will cause it to stop. Often, that is an outside, unplanned action. Or maybe, Mother did plan on calling me into supper which ended my endless playing.

Planning and Agendas

Planning should take place for both planned and unplanned / impromptu events. Some would say that Planning happens during the design phase of an Event. But, Planning needs to continue throughout the entire Event. For events don't always go as planned.

Planning defines what an Event is called and what it does. Planning also defines how an Event fits in with other events.

An Event has an Agenda. This lays out what is supposed to happen during the event. Anyone who has ever led an Event knows that things don't always happen according to the Agenda. In fact, most people know that, even those who have never led an Event.

In a computer, we can control what happens during the Event. Still, sometimes, something will cause things to stray from the Agenda.

In real life, control over Events is just an illusion. We can still put safeguards in place. But, those will only be effective to a certain degree.

When I lead a meeting, I try to go with the flow. When someone starts to veer us off course, I try to gently lead the group back onto the Agenda.

Still, sometimes, that person is not leading us off course. They are instead, leading us where we need to go. When I recognize that that is the case, I quickly modify the Agenda.

Sometimes, it's impossible for *me* to steer a group back onto the Agenda, no matter how important that is. When that's the case, I try to quietly enlist the help of others.

It's usually a surprise when someone leads you off track. Often, I need to have time to analyze what happened. Then, I can decide what to do the next time that happens. I need to step back into Planning.

Handling Errors

If you're using **Hi5ive - Aloha Edition** as an App Building Tool, you'll want to handle Errors such as *File-not-Found, Undefined Variable,* etc.

If you're using **Hi5ive - Aloha Edition** to communicate, the same holds true. However, the Errors might be more like, *What did you say?, What does that mean?. Etc.* As everyone who has ever really tried to communicate knows, misCommunication happens.

To handle Errors in **Hi5ive - Aloha Edition,** you define Conditions. Hopefully, the obvious ones are pre-defined for you. To define the others, use the **Condition** Command.

[**Condition** - Defines a Condition. That Condition can be true or false. That Condition can be set to a Severity-Level - Warning, Error, Severe Error, etc. That Condition can be set to some other Condition like Boiling.]

Condition Condition-Name
  As Condition-Type=Condition-Type
  Options Condition-Options
End-Condition

Sometimes, we can ignore the Condition. At other times, we will have to go back and correct whatever caused that Condition to occur. How much we correct it will depend on several factors including how likely it is that that Condition will happen again. We will also sometimes need to straighten out whatever got messed up when that Condition occurred. And, we might want to change some things to minimize the chance of that ever occurring again.

Conditions can be OK. They can be positive or negative. When positive conditions happen, you might want to celebrate.

When something happens that is not supposed to happen, it might be an error. Or, it might just be a warning. A warning indicates that we should either fix or ignore what happened as needed. Errors, we almost always have to fix. Severe Errors might cause us to scream before we set about fixing them.

A Condition can be of varying degrees. Consider the following Conditions: Boiling, Hot, Warm, Tepid, Cool, Cold, Freezing.

After an App does something or after we communicate something, we can check a Condition. Then, we can perform a Routine based on that Condition. Every Command in **Hi5ive - Aloha Edition** has a **Status** Attribute. We can check that to find out what Condition occurred and where.

```
Copy Structure-A
  To File-A
End-Copy

If Copy.Status = End-of-File
  Then
    Perform End-of-File-Routine
    End-Perform
End-If
```

Knowing this information might not be enough. We might need to trace what happened further upstream. Perhaps, something else precipitated this Condition happening. Yet, no Condition occurred or was reported then.

Consider a Divide by Zero Error. The Error occurred when the App tried to divide something by Zero. Yet, that might not be the real error. The real error might have occurred when that App set that something to Zero.

Tracking Communications

During Projects, Communications might need to be tracked. IMHO, tracking should be used for the purpose of capturing what needs to be captured.

How do we define what needs to be captured? That can get very involved and is probably beyond the scope of this book.

Example of Following Up on Communication that was Tracked:

Our notes say that you're moving and you want the power to your house shut off on Thursday. Is that correct?

Was that Communication effective? How could it have been more effective?

Was it quick? Sometimes, quick is not good. Sometimes, quick means that assumptions were made, rather than figuring out the correct answers.

Did we track the information correctly? Did we track enough information? Did the previous Communication just into one ear and out of the other?

Did this Feedback Communication accomplish what it set out to accomplish? Did we know all of the questions that we needed to ask? Was everything answered thoroughly enough?

Were people assigned to return with answers to the unanswered questions? Do we need to communicate again in order to work through the remaining questions or to finish solving the problem? Who's going to verify the answers?

What if we still have unanswered questions? Who else can we ask? How can we find out those answers? Are some questions better left unanswered?

Often, a checklist can be used to track the Communication. This might include the questions and answers and who asked and answered them.

That checklist might also include the following:

- *Was the question asked?*
- *Was it understood?*
- *Was it answered?* Rather than, *Was an answer given?*

Often the answer to *Was the Communication effective?* is really a different question. *Did I listen?* or *Did I listen well enough?*

Well, I guess there really is a lot to Communication after all, even when you keep it basic.

Exploring Intermediate Communication

As our Communication moves from Basic to Advanced, we tweak it. But, before we can tweak it, we often need to standardize it.

During our standardization, we frequently shorten our Communication. Often, names are the first thing to be shortened. Let's take the word Joseph for instance. We might shorten that to Joe or J.

At the same time, we might expand our Communication. One way that we do this is by adding fluff words. Fluff words add nothing to our Communication other than perhaps beauty or maybe boredom.

We also add ums and ahs. Those give us time to think what we're going to say next. They let the other person(s) know not to interrupt us just yet. We also use um and ah when we need time to remember some particular word that has slipped our mind for the moment.

In order to understand what's being communicated, we rely on pattern recognition.

In order to figure out what's wrong with an App, I also often rely on pattern recognition. Though, in this case, I rely on recognizing when something does *not* match a pattern.

Some of the most difficult patterns to recognize involve multiple negatives. *No, not that, never!*

Another very difficult pattern to interpret is statements or Commands that contain both *and,* and, *or.* Yet, they have no commas or parentheses to indicate how we should interpret them.

A dime and a nickel or a penny.

Is that 1 cent, 11 cents, or 15 cents?

Another pattern that's difficult includes certain letters and numbers. O's and 0's (Oh's and Zero's). In some fonts, those characters are indistinguishable. The same goes for I, l, and 1 – (uppercase i, lowercase L, and the number 1).

IMHO, all fonts for Western Letters should make those distinguishable. They would also not make Q look like 2 or J too similar to I.

Naming Conventions

In **Hi5ive - Aloha Edition,** every object has a name. If we were to define a person, we could say:

Person John
  Is Someone I would like to meet
  Attributes Height = "Tall" Skintone = "Dark" Attractiveness >= "Handsome"
End-Person

But, do we follow a pattern for object names, as most App Building Languages do?

Well, this is a Communications Language. So, we don't have to follow a pattern. Yet, if we're trying to keep our Communication simple or effective, patterns can help.

Below are some patterns that can help. But, just because the might help, that doesn't necessarily mean that you should use them. You'll want to consider how helpful they'll be, how confusing they'll be, and perhaps some other factors.

Do we say **John, JOHN,** or **john?**
Do we say **John Johnson, John-Johnson, JohnJohnson, John_Johnson, John.Johnson,** or **johnJohnson?**
Is it **John Johnson** or **Johnson, John?**

Do we include the object type in the name – **JohnPerson** or **PersonJohn?** That can be helpful, especially when distinguishing a label from a value.

That can also be helpful when naming things at an attribute level, rather than at an object level – **Name.First** for example.

If there are multiple people named John or John Johnson, how do we distinguish them? Maybe we add another attribute value, like **Person-ID:**

Person John
  Is Someone I would like to meet
  Attributes Height = "Tall" Skintone = "Dark" Attractiveness = "Handsome" PersonID=123
End-Person

Alternatively, we could use **Group** and spell out the Relationships of some of those Attribute values.

Group Tall-Handsome-Men
  Parts Person
  Constraints Height="Tall" Attractiveness="Handsome"
End-Group

Only Tall Handsome Men are included in this Group. This makes it easier to find John.

App Building Languages tend to use short names for Object Names. Some of the first App Building Languages only allowed you to use six or maybe eight characters for an Object Name.

So, part of the reason that App Builders use short names when they build Apps is that using short names was sometimes imposed. The rest of the reason they do that is because short names are easier to remember. Programmers also frequently shorten parts of a name in addition to the entire name.

On the other hand, short names are also easier to confuse. Because of that, shortening a name is sometimes more of an art than a science. A dictionary / list of names and words that you have shortened can help.

It helps when everyone who's involved in a Communication follows the same naming conventions. It also helps when everyone calls the same thing by the same name.

IMHO, object names are easiest to remember when they're made up of three or four names. I usually add a two character prefix to indicate the major system involved. Like **GL-Acct-ID** for **G**eneral **L**edger **Acc**ount **ID** or **CU-Acct-ID** for **Cu**stomer **Acc**ount **ID**.

These days, there are several App Building Languages which do not impose any restrictions on the length of a name. Well, they do have limits. However, thousands or millions of characters makes a name too long to remember.

Hi5ive - Aloha Edition imposes no real restrictions on the length of the name. Also, it does not care whether you use - or _ (or some other symbol) as a name separator. Nevertheless, it helps to be consistent.

Let's consider the following names for the same object – your phone number at work:

- **PhoneWork**
- **Phone-Work**
- **Phone_Work**
- **Phone Work**

In **PhoneWork**, there is no separator between parts of the name. That's OK. However, if you use **phonework** without any capital letters, it can at times become hard to know where one word ends and the next word begins.

That probably would not happen in this case. Still, it does happen. And, somebody could read **phonework** as **pho new ork**. You're right! Probably not! Still, there are some situations where something like that is more likely to occur.

Phone-Work. How do we know that **Phone** and **Work** are parts of the Object Name? How do we know that each isn't an object name in and of themselves? If they are, this might be **Phone** minus **Work.** That makes no sense. So, probably not.

Still, let's not confuse ourselves or a computer. Let's surround all mathematical and logical operators with spaces. So, **Phone** minus **Work** would be **Phone – Work**.

Here is that last example that I'll illustrate on Naming Conventions. It's an example of an object name whose parts are separated by a space. **Phone Work.**

How many spaces are allowed? Does it matter? This is by far the most confusing naming convention. Yet, it might be the one that we really want to use. Still, for the sake of Communication, we might want to avoid it.

Other separators can be used, For instance: a period. But, usually, everything that can be easily typed and is not a letter or number, has some other use, except for underscore.

You can resort to using two characters as a separator, so long as that doesn't already have some other meaning. ## or ^#^ for example.

Also, is Phone Work the name of one object or two? You could use ^**Phone Work**^ or something similar. But, if you're going to do that, you might as well use Phone-Work.

Patterns and Pattern Recognition

Communication is all about being able to recognize patterns. That might not be easily recognizable by looking at the English Language. But, patterns are still there. They are just perhaps more muted.

Overlaying / augmenting a Human Language or parts of a Human Language with **Hi5ive - Aloha Edition** makes the patterns more recognizable. And, this can speed up Communication.

Note: I'm not suggesting replacing or overshadowing any Human Language. I'm only suggesting that when we need to see patterns, looking at a Human Language through a Communication Language like **Hi5ive - Aloha Edition** can be very helpful.

The same extends to a project and to all Communication about that project. When we make the patterns stick out, it is easier to bring people up to speed. It also helps them stay on track.

The most obvious pattern in both editions of **Hi5ive,** is that every statement is ended with an **End-.... Define** is ended by an **End-Define. If** is ended by an **End-If.** Etc.

```
Define Object-Name
  As Object-Type=Object-Type
  Options Options [Optional]
End-Define

If Condition
  Then Commands
  Else Commands
End-If
```

Patterns in projects include:

- Overlying pictures or views of the project that show more and more detail.
- Main concepts that apply across various areas of the project. These concepts are often called the same thing across the project. But, sometimes it makes more sense to call them different things when talking to various groups of people.
- Purpose and Approach.

It's easier to recognize patterns when they're highlighted in some way. Yet, patterns in Communication are often subtle. Learning how to recognize them might be an entire Graduate Level Program[22]. This is partly because there's a whole slew of patterns and levels of subtlety.

Facial Recognition can be simplified by only focusing on a few points on the face. Recognizing facial gestures requires a lot more input and analysis. That would be an Advanced Communication Example.

[22] **Pattern Recognition:** My book Solutions Galore covers some pattern recognition and might help you test out of that graduate course.

Positive and Negative Statements

When *NO/NOT* is written, it can be easily overlooked unless it is emphasized in some way. Making it bold and all capital letters is easiest. Underscoring it, making it red, and placing a border around it are other simple options which also emphasize it well.

There are positive statements. There are negative statements. There are statements that are a mixture of both. There are double negatives. And, there are double positives, though those are rare.

Double negatives become positive in App Building Languages. In Communication, we use negatives to emphasize something. The more negatives, the more emphasis. I do this even though I was taught *not* to use *no* double negatives.

When I build Apps, I turn negative statements into positive ones. This makes them more straightforward and less ambiguous. That makes an app easier and quicker to maintain.

App Builders generally don't do that since the positive statement can be longer. I like brevity too. But, if something's confusing or could be confusing, I would rather it be clear.

The same holds true for when I communicate. And, then, I would also rather be positive.

When communicating about your project, are you going to use negatives? If you are:

- How will you emphasize them to make them noticeable?
- What will a negative mean? What will a double negative mean?
- What words / phrases / etc. are negative? Are they always negative?

Also, would somebody please tell me what a wan smile is? Is it a smile or isn't it? How can a smile not be curved upwards?

Smiles are supposed to be positive. At least that's what I always thought until I came across the phrase, *she gave him a wan smile*.

Shortcuts

A shortcut by any other name[23] is still a shortcut. In Communication, shortcuts include acronyms and other types of abbreviations; shorter synonyms; conjunctions; missing, but implied words; and more.

App Builders, myself included, like to take shortcuts.[24] I often create shortcuts for Microsoft Word and Excel. Those shortcuts allow me to work faster in those Apps. I just press a button and lots of work is done on my behalf.

So, **Hi5ive – Aloha Edition** should possibly provide or allow for some shortcuts. On the other hand, for things to be clear, it can be helpful to dissuade the use of shortcuts. I think that the better approach is to make it clear and fairly obvious what each shortcut does.

Concise is what we're looking for. Concise means comprehensive, short, and clear. So long as keeping things concise is included as a rule for your Communication, you should be fine.

Your cheat sheet of all the shortcuts that are OK to use might include the following information. That should make it both concise and clear:

- The name of the shortcut
- A short description of what the shortcut does and possibly why it was given that name
- A quick way to remember the shortcut [optional]
- An example or two of how the shortcut should be used

---

[23] **Other Words for Shortcut:** https://www.merriam-webster.com/thesaurus/shortcut

[24] When it comes to **building Apps, Shortcuts** are sometimes called Macros. I also sometimes call them Hacks.

- An example or two of how the shortcut should not be used
- How you would communicate what you're trying to communicate if you weren't using this shortcut? [optional]

Routines are basically shortcuts. With no Routines, each Command in a **Pookay** or an App would be much longer. You would have to spell everything out every time.

Still, once a shortcut for a set of Commands is introduced, once steps are skipped because they are implied, we might tend to forget to make things clear.

When things are no longer clear, a Language might become stagnant. Then, it falls out of favor, becomes used less and less, until it dies.

The lack of keeping things clear is not the only reason why a Language might die. Another reason is because people are dissuaded from using it. Or, at least, they are not encouraged to use it.

The bottom line is that wisdom is called for when using shortcuts. They can be useful for Communication. They might mean that a Communication can end on time.

Overusing them, though, can lead to forgetting what they mean or do. And, that might, over time, make a Communication meaningless.

It might mean that a Communication is not understood as clearly as it needs to be.

It can also mean that the Communication is understood to mean something other than what the Communicator meant.

Exploring Advanced Communication

Advanced Communication includes Organization, Relationships, Thoughts, Feelings, and more.

Organization

We can organize things fairly easily, though almost everyone has their own ideas about how things should be organized.

Organizing people is more complex. There's the aforementioned various ideas of what Organization means. The Dynamics and Interactions of Groups, and especially of Teams, also come into play.

Organizing cats is even more complex. We sometimes hear about Horse Whisperers[25]. Cat Whisperers? Not so much.

Relationships

On the surface, there are simple relationships and more complex ones.

Simple relationships are things like, *All of my siblings are my sisters* – true story.

More complex relationships are, *My Grandpa's nephew was five years older than my Grandpa* – also a true story.

Relationships run much deeper than the surface. Sometimes, they're stronger than iron. Sometimes, they become volatile.

[25] **Horse Whisperers** can often get Horses to do what they want just by talking to them.

Thoughts

Thoughts, as well as other types of Advanced Communications, require descriptions. Thoughts are much more complex than speech. Still speech often contains unspoken thoughts.

Example:

Sure, I love you!
[Thought: *Though, there are times ....*]

Feelings

Feelings lie just deeper than thoughts. Sometimes, we call them Emotions. But, what we call Emotions might only be the labels that we try to assign to our Feelings.

Usually, our Feelings are vague. How do you communicate something that's vague?

Organization

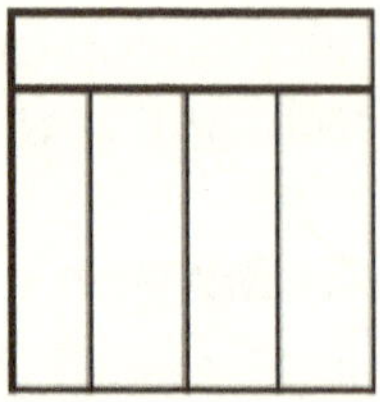

Organization is frequently hierarchical, even if we are just organizing the silverware drawer. My silverware drawer always contains an organization bin (something with various compartments). [Sometimes, I have to make that organization bin myself.]

What goes in the right-most compartment of your silverware drawer organizer? For those who are right-handed, that's the compartment you'll probably reach for first. So, you might want to place what you will most likely want to retrieve in the right-most compartment. At the same time, there's some unwritten rule, or maybe it's written in a kitchen etiquette book, that spoons go in the right-hand compartment.

What type of silverware do I use the most? Spoons. So, it's convenient that spoons go in that right-hand compartment. However, I'm 99% certain that spoons go there because that's the way I was raised. And, it's what I'm used to. Also, that's what the etiquette book said was proper. On top of that, my wife says that's where they go.

I'm ambidextrous. So, for me, spoons could go anywhere.

In the kitchen in this house, however, the right-most compartment of the silverware drawer is always the easiest one to reach.

The left-most compartment is too close to the counter. If I use my left-hand to grab silverware, I have to make certain that I stand far enough away from that counter. Otherwise, I'll bump my hand on it. And, that usually hurts.

Organization in Companies is often communicated through Org Charts. [These are also called Org*anization* Charts and

Organization*al* Charts.] See Information Reports and Charts in the Information Communication Examples section above for more information on Charts in general.

In an Org Chart for a Company, the Board and/or CEO is at the top. At the bottom might be whatever the company considers to be the lowest level workers, possibly Interns.

However, Org Charts often only show the highest levels of Employees. When that's the case, the bottom of those Org Charts show the lowest level of those highest level Employees. When Org Charts show Employees at levels below Manager, they might only show the role / job title and not the name or the actual Employee.

So, whoever's creating the Org Chart needs to understand who is to appear on the Org Chart. They also need to understand where and how each person is to appear on the Org Chart.

(Thinking more about those Org Charts, one might put the most important Employees first. Those might be the lowest-level workers. Or, it might be the top-performing employees. Or, it might be those producing the most revenue for the company. This would mean that your pay rate would be taken into consideration.)

Various Company Websites show the Top Employees on their About Page. This Chart typically only shows boxes without the connecting lines. Also, usually, any there hierarchical placement of the boxes is not so apparent. Each box has a picture of the employee (or their avatar). Their bio appears to the right or below that picture.

My book series, The Wizard Without a Wand has ten main Characters. I created a webpage[26] to display each main Character's picture and their bio.

---

[26] **The Wizard without a Wand Cast of Characters Webpage:** https://stubbart.com/publishing_consulting/cast/wizardwithoutawand.html

When you first look at this webpage, you only see their picture, name, and role. When you click on a picture, it rotates and shows you a short bio of that character. Click on their bio to show only their picture, name, and title again.

There are a variety of ways to show a Chart about Employees. All of those Charts are basically Org Charts. And, Org Charts are the, IMHO, easiest way to communicate who your Employees are and what they do.

To be honest though, I'm usually not looking at Org Charts on a Company's website in order to see the CEO's or anybody else's credentials, I'm looking at it to see if this is a Company that I would like to work for.

- Are the people smiling? Are they fake smiling?
- Do they all have to dress up? Will this Company be more interested in my appearance than they are in what I can do for them?
- Are there a variety of people? Or are they all men or perhaps all young?
- Are they all young? Will a kupuna (senior, older person) like me be accepted into that group? [In kupuna, the u's are pronounced as oo. The a is pronounced as a short a.]

Sequencing

Sequencing puts things into some sort of order.
Some Sequences are time-based. Some are not based on time.
Sequences might be in alphabetical or categorical order.
Sequences might be arranged in some other type of Sequence.
Sequenced can be randomized or shuffled, rather than ordered.

Many sequences involve both a time-based sequence and a non-time-based Sequence. When this occurs, the overall sequence is usually described as though it's time-based or not. Usually, these are referred to as time-based when the highest-level sequence is time-based.

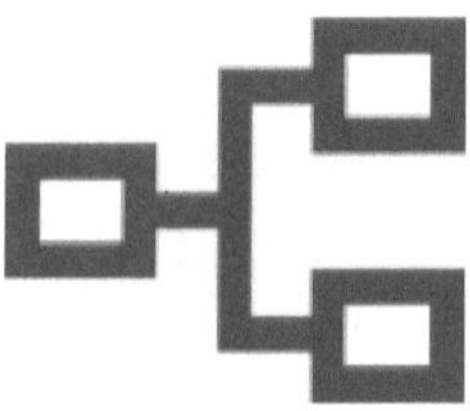

Sequences are often visualized with Flowcharts [Type of Diagram]. And, Sequences are often called *Flows,* regardless of how well they flow. A Flowchart can often help us see how to make sequences flow better.

Parallelism refers to doing multiple things at the same time. In other words, those things happen in parallel. Parallelism is often used to speed things up. This definition of Parallelism has nothing to do with dimensions.

When Parallelism occurs, the corresponding Flowchart often splits into multiple Flowcharts. Unfortunately, that makes it easier for one of those flows to get overlooked, forgotten, or assigned a lower level of importance than is warranted.

Sometimes, the only thing that is done to improve the speed of a Sequence of events, is to Thread it. [Split it into Parallel events.]

Other [non-thread-related] improvements for speed should be applied first. Then, that event can be Threaded. Sometimes, when those improvements aren't made, Threading doesn't improve the speed of a process that much.

The only processes or events that can be split off and run in Parallel, are those that are not dependent on each other.

For instance, today, everyone received a raise. So, you need to change all of the salaries before you run payroll. Not only do you need to change the salaries first, you can't change salaries while you're running payroll and vice-versa. So, you can't run those two things in parallel.

Relationships

When I was young, my older sister knew <u>everything</u> about relationships within our family. She taught me who my cousins were. She taught me who my first and second cousins were. Then, she tried to teach me who my first cousins once-removed were. And, that's when it started to make less sense.

Sure, I could follow the diagrams and figure things out. Yet, I was looking for there to be more to relationships than what a diagram could tell me. I was looking for depth.

Diagrams can tell you how people are related. They're not so good at telling you why they're related or why they remain related. The why's can become abstract very fast. And, maybe, things like love and attraction don't need to be diagrammed. Maybe, they just need to be felt.

Still, diagrams can be useful to figure out what we expect out of relationships. They can point out instances where relationships might fail. They might help us see the invisible *Do Not Cross* lines.

Diagrams can also help us see what it will take to repair various breaks in relationships. Though sometimes, one person in a relationship might say, *If I have to spell it out, it's not worth it.* Or, *If I have to spell it out, it's not the same.*

How do we deal with things that I should know, but you will never tell me? How do we deal with things that I'll forget, yet, I don't want you to remind me about them?

What's the equation for trust?

How do we Communicate about how we Interact with others? We can interact over the phone or over a video call. We might use an App on our laptop or phone to text someone else. We can communicate by email or snail mail.

We can communicate in person. And, if our Interaction with them involves more than Communication, it's often helpful to get together in person.

Often our Relationships are not well-delineated. Sometimes, they're downright fuzzy. When that happens we need to adjust our rules of Communication so that we can all communicate more deeply.

Thoughts and Beyond

Thoughts can be words that we don't say out loud. They're only in our heads. Still, those thoughts are words.

As we let go of words, our thoughts can become pictures. Often, the best way to communicate a picture is with the picture itself.

Along with the picture, we can communicate what type of art it is. However, what most people are looking for is the subject of the picture and other people's impressions. So, we can communicate those things also.

All of those things can be attributes of the picture. Just like a name is an attribute of a person.

Thoughts can get fuzzy. We might need to add *almost* and *is-close-to* to **Hi5ive - Aloha Edition** to handle those thoughts.

Example #1: The creature that I was thinking of was almost a bear.

```
Copy Bear
  To Creature-I-Was-Thinking-Of
  Through Almost
End-Copy
```

Example #2: This is the Creature I was thinking of, maybe.

```
If This-Animal is-close-to Bear
  Then
    Copy This-Animal
      To Creature-I-Might-Have-Been-Thinking-Of
    End-Copy
End-If
```

We can move beyond the place where Thoughts are pictures. We can move into a world without [the need for] language. Martha Beck and others calls this *The Wordless Wonder* or *Wordlessness*[27].

Communication still happens in that space. I find that when I get in contact with beauty and wonder, I often let go of words and drop into a space where things are communicated in thoughts or pictures. The same thing happens when I communicate with nature and with the spiritual world. Sometimes, even the pictures and thoughts drop away. But, there is still communication. It's hard to describe. I just know things.

It might be the case that the only way to communicate what you experience in The Wordless Wonder is to have another person have an experience there. Theirs might be a different experience. Still, people who have this type of experience are often more able to understand another person's experience of this type. [That might be true of all sorts of experiences.]

It's not that **Hi5ive - Aloha Edition** can't be used for this type of Communication. What it means is that new Routines, **Pookay, HakaPookay,** and other things might need to be introduced. Things beyond pictures and fuzzy logical operators like is-close-to.

Perhaps, we would introduce *Understand, Kythe (Show your true self to another*[28]*), Communion (a type of Sharing that goes beyond understanding and knowledge), Sharing Aloha, etc.*

Whatever we do, **Hi5ive - Aloha Edition** is made up of words. So, it's hard to express something that is totally wordless

---

[27] **Wordlessness:** https://marthabeck.com/2013/08/doing-nothing/

[28] **Kythe:** https://www.thewellspring.com/flex/professional-integration/2463/kything-being-present-to-another.cfm.html

with it. Still, **Hi5ive - Aloha Edition** can help us communicate a wordless experience.

We can express:

- What occurred multiple times in that experience? What patterns exist?
- What were the main points?
- What were your feelings before, during, and after that experience?

Hi5ive - Original Edition breaks down an App Building Language to its basic Commands. Likewise, you can break down a wordless experience to its basic components. You can then combine those components to reflect your larger experience.

Sometimes the most extraordinary things can be explained simply. And, that's perhaps when we understand them the best.

Sharing stories can help.

Feelings

How do we communicate squishy ooshy feelings? We can try to assign a label to them:

- Fear
- Joy
- Sadness
- Giddiness
- Anger
- Contentedness
- Rage
- Excitement
- Etc. Yes, that etc. feeling. You know, the one that's impossible to label.

Nevertheless, none of those labels, even combined, gets across the fulness of the feeling.

The best way to communicate a feeling is to let it express itself. Though, in the cases of rage and anger, other attempts to communicate it might serve us better. At the same time, it is not good to quash feelings. But, letting those two out in the proper place and time might prove to be prudent.

Perhaps we could communicate our feelings better if we had more complete labels. There's nothing wrong with those that we currently use. It's just that they only start to convey what we're feeling. Perhaps, we need to add some qualities to the label.

Let's take happiness for example. One quality of happiness is exuberance. Actually, it's the level of exuberance.

It's just like when I'm looking for a place to stay. I might look for a three-star hotel. When I'm overjoyed with my stay there, how many stars do I give to my level of exuberance? Hopefully, I give it at least three.

Other qualities of happiness also come with their own levels. Some qualities of happiness are expressed externally. The rest are expressed internally whether the person who's experiencing the happiness is aware of them or not.

There are times when feelings are nebulous. At least, that's the way it works for many people.

We need something else in **Hi5ive – Aloha Edition** for nebulousness. We use = for equal. Nebulous is somewhat equal. We can, perhaps, use ~ [approximate] for nebulous.

But, how approximate is approximate? Is it maybe, perhaps, possibly, probably, almost definitely, a mere chance, within the same degree of magnitude,[29] nebulous, or some other distance from equal?

Perhaps **?=** or **???** would be a better symbol for nebulousness. The latter symbol could be modified by adding or subtracting ? to indicate the degree of nebulousness.

In some App Building Languages, there are two kinds of equal. The most common kind is equal in value.

The other type is equal in value and in ever other aspect. A human child and a dog are both five years old. However a human child is not a dog. Nor, is a dog a human child.

When App Building Languages look at *all* aspects of equal, they are looking at:

- Are the values equal?

---

[29] **Degree of Magnitude** is also called Order of Magnitude: https://en.wikipedia.org/wiki/Order_of_magnitude

- Do both values contain the same type of value [usually numeric or text]?

For human Communication, we consider two things as being equal when enough things about them are equal. *Enough*, is another nebulous term. We might need one or more operators to represent different varieties of *nebulous*.

Exploring Complex Communication

Feelings can be complex, especially when they seem foreign.

Still, I prefer to think of feelings as an advanced form of Communication. I like to think that feelings also segue into a complex form of Communication. I don't know if there is a namr for that. Still, feelings themselves aren't quite that complex.

As we explore Complex Communication, let's look at the lifecycle of Communication first.

Then, we'll look at Subconscious Expressions.

Next, we'll look at the Dynamic Interactions that can happen when you're part of a Team.

Music and Art can be very complex. Combine them, and you might have Dance.

The Lifecycle of Communication

We can look at the Lifecycle of Communication as beginning with a Concept and ending with something Concrete.

Concepts

How do we communicate Concepts? What is a Concept?

One way to explain a Concept is to break it down into its various parts. But, don't forget the Organizations, Sequences, and Relationships. Those are also parts of the Concept. And, the Concept is more than all of its parts.

Another way to explain a Concept is to begin with a similar Concept. Then, we can explain how those Concepts are similar and how they're different.

Ideas to Inventions

Concepts are Ideas. You might start out with part of an Idea. You keep adding parts until you have the entire Idea, or at least the major part of the Idea.

Once you have your Idea, you try to turn it into an Invention. Your Idea is in your mind. The Invention is your Idea in your hands. Your Idea is mental. The Invention is usually physical.

If successful, your Invention will do what you thought your Idea would do. But, you can't be certain of that until you create a successful Invention.

Most of the time, our Invention will not be exactly the same as our Idea said it would be. Due to technical difficulties and limitations, our Invention is often slightly different than how we envisioned it. Sometimes, it's not at all like the result that we stated with our Idea. Yet, it started out life *as* our Idea.

Communication's Life Cycle

Communication usually goes from thoughts to spoken or written words. Rarely does Communication end. That's because it keeps spawning new thoughts and Ideas. And, attempts will be made to turn some of those Ideas into Inventions.

You might be able to draw a chart showing how your Idea became an Invention. Unless we document the entire process as it happens, most of us will forget some of the events that helped the result turn into a successful Invention.

But, what about the transition from an Invention to your next Idea. That's a little harder to chart. It's especially hard when we think that our Idea spawned from nothing.

Perhaps, the Universe placed that Idea in our mind. I think that most of the time, our Idea is based upon an Invention that was based upon an Idea, etc. We just don't realize it happened that way.

Feedback Loops

In Science, there's a thing called a *Feedback Loop*. Something from the end product is fed into the start of a sequence. And, the sequence starts all over again.

Complete loops are Sequences. Yet, when that loop varies, it becomes a Complex Sequence. [See the Sequencing chapter in the previous section for more information on Sequences.] The restart point might vary. The new Idea might be quite different from the previous Idea.

Let's call the Lifecycle of Communication an *Endless Complex Loop*. It's very complex, because often, we've got multiple Communications going on at the same time. We're turning multiple Ideas into Inventions simultaneously.

And, often, we don't completely turn many of those Ideas into Inventions. Some, we continue to develop them further. Others fall away from our focus.

As for Communications, completing them is often not the point. Rather, the point might be making sure that they never end.

Deep Dives into Ideas

Sometimes, the purpose of a Communication is to further explore an Idea. We want to look at it more deeply. We might want to break it down into smaller chunks.

There are times when we use Communication to get a better handle on something.

We can define it in more concrete terms.

Alternatively, we can look at that something in more abstract or generic terms. Explaining something in generic terms can be helpful when we're trying to explain something to someone who doesn't think in the terms that we're used to using to express it.

Subconscious Expressions

Words are one form of verbal expression. Yet, we might throw in an *um* or an *ah*.

We might pause.

Our voice might give way or crack or go wild.

Sometimes those things just happen. But, usually, when they happen, our subconscious is trying to communicate things. In my case, those last mean that I should stop trying to communicate for a while. I'm tired and a need a break from that. At least, I need to stop trying to communicate vocally.

How do we communicate what our subconscious is trying to say?

Let's start with *um* and *ah*. These are filler words.[30] They also go by other names – see the Reference Note. Sometimes, we use actual words like *like* as filler words, rather than vocalizations including *um* and *ah*.

We use filler words in order for it to continue to be our turn while our mind catches up and figures out what we want to say next. We're pausing, but we don't want others to think that its their turn to speak. So, we throw in something to fill that pause.

I have yet to master this. Others often think I'm done, rather than just pausing. So, they start speaking.

Do people always use the same filler word? Is there some pattern to when they use different ones or is it all just random?

[30] **Filler Words:** https://en.wikipedia.org/wiki/Filler_(linguistics)

If anybody could answer those questions, we might be able to better understand what that person is saying and why they're pausing. We might get a clue about what their subconscious is trying to communicate, if it's trying to communicate anything other than, *It's still my turn to speak.*

Um is not just a vocalized pause. There are signs for *Um* in American Sign Language.

Um might indicate that it's going to take me longer to figure out what to say.

Ah might indicate a brief pause. Perhaps, I'm coming up for air.

Then, again, *Um* and *Ah* might indicate something else. Or, they might not indicate anything at all.

Perhaps, we wouldn't have to rely on *um* and *ah* if we knew that we had a certain amount of time to speak. That might work for giving a speech in public. It usually doesn't work for political debates.

Some people often *speak with their hands,* even when they're not using Sign Language. At least, they make a lot of gestures with their hands and arms while they're speaking.

Sometimes, these gestures add extra meaning or emphasis to what's being said.

Sometimes, they're more like *um* and *ah* or *whatever.*

If we're really trying to understand what's being communicated we should develop some method of categorizing what those different gestures mean. However, they might just be random. It might be that any gesture can mean anything. If that's the case, it might be meaningless to try to categorize them.

I know that I use hand gestures to help me figure out what I want to say. They help me figure out the correct word. I suspect that the same is true for some others.

Sometimes, my hands are creating an abstract 3D image of the word. Sometimes, they're pulling the word from my brain to my mouth. I usually have no idea what my hand gestures mean. And, probably, neither does anyone else.

On the other hand, we often quickly recognize facial gestures. We usually recognize them subconsciously, rather than consciously.

We could give more depth to some audio recordings of people speaking, if we included a translation of their facial gestures.

However, some people use more facial expressions than others. And, I suspect that different people use facial expressions differently, especially, when they're from different cultures.

Perhaps, we also subconsciously interpret hand gestures. They might mean something. Or, they might put what's being said into context.

Let's look at how we might gain more insight about what the subconscious is trying to communicate.

Pretend that we just led a brainstorming session. People were throwing out ideas left and right. Now, we want to go back and look more deeply at some of those ideas.

We bring in a person who was putting forth an idea, and we replay the video recording of what they said. They can write down more depth and information during the playback.

Then, we play the recording back a second time. This time, we ask them to pay close attention to the filler words and gestures they used. Again, if more comes to them, they should write that down or otherwise mention it.

That's probably more useful than trying to assign certain meanings to certain filler words and/or gestures.

For spoken / written words, we have dictionaries and thesauri. There are also Encyclopedias of Gestures, and to a lesser extent, of Filler Words. And, those can be useful when the gesture means the same thing to many people.

But, sometimes, a filler word is just a pause and a gesture is just a gesture. When that's the case, it's easier to understand what's being communicated when we filter them out.

If we were to capture filler words and gestures in **Hi5ive - Aloha Edition,** we would probably treat them as attributes.

Team Dynamics

I used to call Team Dynamics, *Group Dynamics*. They are still the Dynamics of a Group. However, they come into play and are visible more often when that Group acts together as a Team.

The better that Team works together *as* a Team, the more these Team Dynamics come into play. Working together as a Team also helps those Dynamics come into play more easily.

Team Dynamics are positive Group Dynamics. There are also negative Group Dynamics. Those can turn a Group and maybe even a Team against itself.

How many is enough?

Sometimes you can be a team all by yourself. You can communicate between your various selves.

The more that your various selves are friends with each other, the happier they'll be. And, they'll be able to communicate more easily.

Sometimes a Team of two or three enjoys the benefits of Team Dynamics. Usually, though, the full benefits of Team Dynamics kick in when the Team grows to somewhere between 12 to 20 people.

My definition of Team Dynamics says that when there's a Team of sufficient size, there are always enough willing people who are available to accomplish the major goals of the team. You might need an Organizational Chart in order to see this.

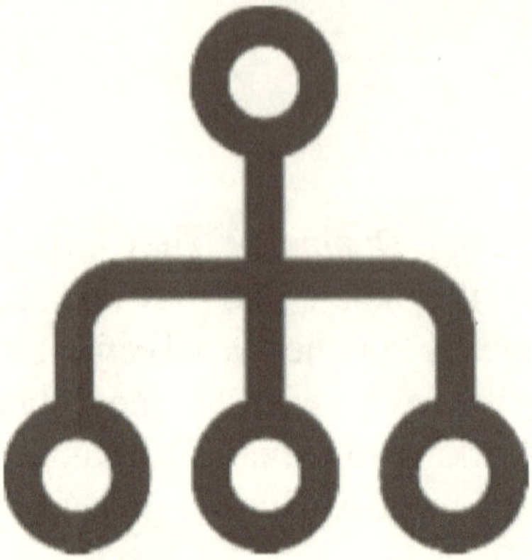

Imagine that this Org Chart, not only shows names and roles of various people on the Team. Imagine that it also shows how each role will help the Team accomplish their major goals. Perhaps, that would be written in a list off to the side of the diagram.

There might be a Team Member who intuitively or through their knowledge of people on the Team, knows who might be willing and able to perform a certain task or role. That person might or might not perform that task every time. Sometimes people on the Team will volunteer for a task or role.

Small Teams can often perform the same tasks as large Teams. And, they can often perform them more efficiently.
Larger Teams, on the other hand, might lead to more interactions. And, perhaps *that's* what you're looking for.
Both approaches can lead to efficiently accomplishing tasks. However, it seems like it's easier for very large Groups to tend to become unwieldly. They need to do more to remain a Team.

Music

Programmed Music has been around for over 100 years.

In 1896, Edwin Votey invented the Pianola.[31] The Pianola was a player piano. Later on, player pianos were generically called *pianolas*.

Player Pianos operate by turning a spool to make music. The spool has knobs or notches that tell pianolas which notes to play. More information on how they work is at the link in the previous reference note.

So, even though there was no computer involved, these player pianos were programmed. Want a different song? Insert a different spool / program / App / **Pookay.**

Even though many people don't know how to make Music with their computer, it's still doable. Just search the Internet for *Virtual Piano* to get started. You'll be presented with online Apps for playing Music using your Computer keyboard.

These days, the relationship of Computers to Music is usually more along the lines of using a Computer as a Music Studio to combine various recordings / riffs. You might still play Music. However, usually, you're not playing it one key at a time. You're probably playing one song or part of a song at a time.

In order to use **Hi5ive - Aloha Edition** to play Music or to describe playing Music, we would need to add a **Play** Command. Let's base it on the **Perform** Command.

Music is often complex. It is more than playing the correct notes in the correct order for the correct length of time. So, let's say that

[31] **The Pianola:** https://en.wikipedia.org/wiki/Player_piano

we've written a lot of Routines in **Hi5ive - Aloha Edition** that are related to Music. We now have so many of these Routines, that we've stored them in a **HakaPookay** called **LeoOLeho.** More information is below (after the **Play** Command).

[**LeoOLeho.Play** - Plays Music]
LeoOLeho.Play Performer-Name
Using Parameters
Looping Conditions
LeoOLeho.End-Play

LeoOLeho is short for Ka Leo O Ka Leho. [The a's are pronounced as short a's. The e's are pronounced as long a's. The o's are pronounced as long o's.] That's Hawaiian for *The Sound of the Shell*. Sung music in Hawaiian is Mele. Instrumental Music is Pila Ho'okani. I could have used Kani for any sound. I chose **LeoOLeho** instead.

There might be a **HalePookay** called **Kani.** Within that Library, there's probably a **HakaPookay** / Bookshelf called **Mele** and another called **PilaHo'okani.** In **Mele,** there is no **Play** Command. Rather, there is a **Sing** Command. The **Play** Command would be in **PilaHo'okani.**

I wanted something more generic. I wanted the **Play** Command to be able to use Parameters. Those Parameters would include:

- What is to be played
- The instrument(s) that is (are) to play it. In the case of singing, that instrument would be the voice.

All of that led me to use LeoOLeho instead.

My mother was a great pianist. She often accompanied people who were singing or who were playing other instruments. However, her Piano Music was written in one key and the Music for the other person was usually written in a different key. That is, the Music for the piano was either higher or lower than the Music for the other instrument or the singer.

Sometimes, my mother played duets with another pianist. Usually, then, the Music was written in the same key.

When the Music was written in a different key, my mother would have to Transpose her Music to match the other person's. Sometimes, the other person could Transpose their Music to match my mother's. But, piano's can play a wider range of Music. So, transposing Music for a Piano is more often possible than for another instrument or someone else's voice. And, besides, my mother was good at it. I think she might have even liked transposing Music.

To accomplish Musical Transposition in **Hi5ive - Aloha Edition,** we can use the **Copy** Command. Let's say that **LeoOLeho** contains a **Transform** Routine.

```
Copy Original-Piece-of-Music
  To Transposed-Piece-of-Music
  Through LeoOLeho.Transform(C#, Down, A)
End-Copy
```

C#, Down, A tells the Transform Routine to shift the original piece of Music from the key of C# down to the key of A. We could include the number of octaves[32] to shift the Music, along with **Down/Up.** So, **C#, Down 0, A** would shift the music down to **A. C#, Down 1, A** would shift the music down one octave [**For example:** C would get shifted down to the next C] and then down to the key of **A.**

[32] **Octave:** From one C to the next C is one octave (8 notes). We can replace both Cs with any key and it will still be one octave.

Or, perhaps, **LeoOLeho** contains a **Transpose** Command.

[**Transpose** - Transposes a piece of music.]
Transpose Piece-of-Music
  <u>To</u> Piece-of-Music
  <u>Through</u> Transposition
End-Transpose

Transpose has a different meaning in Music, than it does with letters, numbers, or words. In those cases, **Transpose** would mean to reposition.

In Music, we are swapping the notes from one key to the other. So, I guess that the meanings are somewhat similar. It's just that **Transpose** in Music is more complex.

Art

There are several forms of Art[33] including Visual Art, Writing, and Music. I'm guessing that the complete list is as long as our creativity is wide.

Hi5ive - Aloha Edition helps us communicate about Visual Art. The **Draw, Feature, Segment, Shape, Style,** and **Theme** Commands were all created with Visual Art in mind. **Layout** can also be very useful for Visual Art. Those and the rest of the Commands can also be used when you're creating any kind of Art.

I suspect that there's an **Art HalePookay.** We can call it Hana No'eau which means *artwork*. [The a's in Hana are short *a's*. The o in No'eau is a long o. The ' is a glottal stop and separates the o from e. The e is pronounced like a long *a*. The au is pronounced by saying those vowels together (short *a* and *oo*. au is almost pronounced like *ow*. So, Hana No|ayau. Though ayau is probably run together somewhat.]

That **HanaNo'eau HalePookay** might contain the basic Commands for creating Art. But, it no doubt goes beyond that and does more. **HanaNo'eau** contains a **HakaPookay** for each type of Art.

---

[33] **Forms of Art:** https://www.aardvarkartservices.com/what-are-the-7-major-forms-of-art/ That reference lists seven. There are more. https://www.britannica.com/topic/the-arts lists ten. Both references list Writing as Literature. Are there more? Probably. I notice that Paperfolding (including Origami) is not on the list.

When I hear the term *Art,* I first think of Visual Art. I think of Painting, Coloring, Charcoal, and Photography. Those and perhaps other types of Visual Art are 2D Visual Art.[34]

There's also 3D Visual Art. That includes Sculpture, most Paper Folding, String Figures, Mobiles, Models, etc.

It would make sense if Visual Art was a **HakaPookay** within **HanaNo'eau.** Within the Visual Art **HakaPookay,** there would be **HakaPookay** of 2D Visual Art and 3D Visual Art. I'll give those **HakaPookay** their Hawaiian names at the end of this chapter.

I'm thinking that the various types of 2D Visual Art are similar enough that no further **HakaPookay** are needed. I'm not sure that's true for 3D Visual Art. After all, 3D Visual Art includes a whole 'nother dimension of complexity.

In this theoretical **HanaNo'eau,** there are basic appearance Commands: **Size, Shape, Resolution,** and Commands to alter the background.

There are Editing Commands and Routines: **Brush, Color, Draw, Fill, Text,** etc. This **Draw** Command draws more than just basic shapes. [That's what **Hi5ive - Aloha Edition's Draw** Command does.]

There are Filter Commands and Routines: **Brightness, Contrast,** and artistic filters (blurs, frames, textures, etc.). There are Commands and Routines to alter the style (**Watercolor, India Ink,** various Artists' styles, etc.). Etc.

---

[34] For a **list of 2D Visual Art** Commands, just open a Photo / Picture Editor on your computer.

Hawaiian Names for Visual Art HakaPookay

Let's call the Visual Art **HakaPookay, *Ki'i'Ike*.**[35] [The i's are pronounced as long *e's*. The ' are glottal stops that separate the i's. The e is pronounced as a long *a*.]

If **2DKi'i'Ike** [Two-Dimensional **Ki'i'Ike**] has a Palette Theme, and you want to change it, precede **Palette-Theme** with **HanaNo'eau.Ki'i'Ike. 2DKi'i'Ike.**

Specifying **HanaNo'eau.Ki'i'Ike.2DKi'i'Ike** all the time can get to be monotonous. And, I'll bet that even if I copy that every time I use it, I'll misspell it at least once.

So, **Hi5ive - Aloha Edition** allows us to define Synonyms. We can do that with the **Synonym** Command.

Synonym Synonym-2D
  As Synonym-Type=Alternate-Name
  Options Reference=**HanaNo'eau.Ki'i'Ike.
2DKi'i'Ike**
End-Synonym

The next chapter will explore the topic of Art some more.

---

[35] In Hawaiian, **Visual Art** is ***ki'i 'ike*** *maka – Mark the seen image*. Maka is mark. So, I left that part off of the name for that **HakaPookay**.

Do It Again!

Creating Visual Art in **Hi5ive - Aloha Edition** can be tedious because it can require many steps. Let's use the **HanaHou HakaPookay.** This **HakaPookay** can take away some of that tediousness by combining some of those steps.

Hana Hou is Hawaiian and Hawaiian Pidgin for *Do it again!* or *Encore!* [In the word Hana, the a's are pronounced as short *a's*. In the word Hou, the ou is pronounced by saying those vowels quickly, one right after the other, so that they slide right together. It is almost pronounced *ow*.]

First, I'll explain how to create a Theme in **Hi5ive - Aloha Edition.** I'll show you why that can be tedious. Then, I'll introduce **HanaHou** and how we can use it to reduce the number of steps and therefore the tediousness of creating a Theme.

Visual Art can be created in many Picture Apps. These Apps contain a Palette. A Palette is a Theme in **Hi5ive - Aloha Edition.** A Theme is a Group of Styles.

In order to create a Theme, the Styles need to be defined. For instance the following Style Command sets the default background and foreground colors:

```
Style Color-Background
  As Style-Type=Color
  Options Color=Azure, Use=Background
End-Style

Style Color-Foreground
  As Style-Type=Color
  Options Color=Midnight-Blue, Use=Foreground-and-
Text
```

End-Style

After defining every Style, group them into the Theme.

Group Palette-Theme
  Parts Attributes-and-their-Default-Values
  Constraints Attribute-and-Overall-Theme-Constraints
End-Group

Palette-Theme is then filled using several **Copy** Commands like the one below:

Copy DarkBlue
  To Palette-Theme.Color-Background
End-Copy

If Paint Brushes, Colored Pencils, etc. are Styles of **Palette-Theme,** specifying all of the attributes could end up being tedious. That would take several **Copy** Commands. Why not copy everything with one **Copy** Command? **HanaHou.Copy** will let us do that.

HanaHou.Copy is a different version of **Hi5ive - Aloha Edition.Copy. Hanahou** also contains different versions of several other **Hi5ive - Aloha Edition** Commands. Mostly, **HanaHou** contains the **Copy** Command and the Commands like **Copy.**

The difference between the **Hi5ive - Aloha Edition.Copy** Command and the **HanaHou** version is that you can copy multiple things to a Group or Definition with just one **HanaHou.Copy** Command. The other **HanaHou** Commands work similarly. That is you only need to execute a Command once, rather than several times.

We could write the **HanaHou.Copy** Command as:

HanaHou.Copy DarkBlue; Transparent(100%); OilPaintBrush; 10px; 12px; Medium; Blend
<u>To</u> Palette-Theme.Color-Foreground; Palette-Theme.Color-Background; Palette-Theme.Drawing-Instrument; Palette-Theme.BrushStrokeWidth; Palette-Theme.BrushStrokeHeight; Palette-Theme.BrushStrokeThickness; Palette-Theme.Merge
HanaHou.End-Copy

But, that's kind of difficult to read. So, let's write it this way instead:

HanaHou.Copy
<u>Destination</u> Palette-Theme
DarkBlue <u>To</u> Color-Foreground
100% <u>To</u> Color-Background <u>Through</u> Transparent-Routine
OilPaintBrush <u>To</u> Drawing-Instrument
10px <u>To</u> Brush-Stroke-Width
12px <u>To</u> Brush-Stroke-Height
Medium <u>To</u> Brush-Stroke-Thickness
Blend-Method <u>To</u> Merge-Method
HanaHou.End-Copy

Change Palette-Theme to **HanaNo'eau.Ki'i'Ike. 2DKi'i'Ike.** Palette-Theme, if that's the Theme that you want to change. Or, if you've created the Synonym Synonym-2D, specify it as Synonym-2D.Palette-Theme.

This easier-to-read version of the **HanaHou** Copy Command is formatted slightly differently from the **Hi5ive - Aloha Edition Copy** Command. At the same time, it looks similar.
There are multiple <u>To</u>'s. There can be a <u>Through</u> for each <u>To</u>.

The Destination Attribute only exists for **HanaHou.**Copy. The Destination can be any Group or Definition.

Placing Destination before all of the To attributes means that you don't have to wade through those before finding out what the Destination is. Placing Destination after all of the To's might seem like a better way to write this. But, it wouldn't help us understand what the Command is doing. At least, it wouldn't help us understand that quite so early on.

Specifying all of the values that need to be set, can get tedious. Yet, the idea behind **Hi5ive - Aloha Edition** is to keep everything simple. So, how do you do that when you're working with complex things?

- Consistency
- Breaking things down into smaller pieces
- Combining things that are generically the same
- Moving multiple steps into Routines so that you don't lose the forest for the trees.
- Moving multiple Routines to **HakaPookay.**

Dance

Dance can be choreographed or freestyle or something in-between. Dance can also be something altogether different.

In almost all of its forms, Dance is a combination of Music and Art. Or, Dance can be said to be Art that is set to Music.

[I'm assuming that there's at least one form of Dance that is not both Music and Art. [That includes Music that is only in the Dancer's head.] Surely, with all of the various forms of Dance, there must be at least one exception. Still, I could be wrong.]

To work with Dance in **Hi5ive - Aloha Edition,** we would need to use the following **HakaPookay:**

- **LeoOLeho (Music)**
- **Ki'i'Ike (Visual Art)**
- **HanaHou (Do it Again)**

For Visual Art, we mostly used **2DKi'i'Ike.** For Dance, we use **3DKi'i'Ike.**

Do we need any other **HakaPookay, Pookay,** Routines, or Commands to express Dance?

We might need a **HakaPookay** for Movement / Animation. We could call it **Ne'ePeki** (Move Step-by-Step). [The e's in **Ne'ePeki** are pronounced as long *a's*. The ' is a glottal stop and separates the first two e's. The i is pronounced as a long *e*.]

We might also need an **Interaction HakaPookay.** Of course, this might be one of those dances where there is no interaction between the Dancers. It might be a Dance where each Dancer does their own thing. In both of those cases we would not need this **HakaPookay.**

We could combine all of those **HakaPookay** into a **Choreography** (**A'oHula**)[36] **HalePookay.** [The a's in **A'oHula** are short *a's*. ' is a glottal stop and separates the a and the o. The o is a long *o*. u is pronounced *oo*.]

Actually, all Interactions in Dance are Movements. So, we don't really need a separate **Interaction HakaPookay.** We just need to expand **Ne'ePeki,** the Movement **HakaPookay** to include those types of Movements.

Let's take a look at **Ne'ePeki.** Movements / Animations can involve:

- Moving objects
- Transitioning objects to other objects
- Rotating objects
- Formatting objects – Shading; Fading: Changing Color, Font, Font-Style; Highlighting; etc.
- Transitions
- Enhancing, degrading objects
- Morphing objects – Changing Age, Hair, Clothing, Species, etc. And, morphing objects from one into another.
- Making objects interact with other objects

Animations can happen almost instantly or over a long period of time. Multiple Animations can happen at the same time.

Let's take a look at Interactions some more. Interactions happen between objects. Yes, an object can interact with itself. A Dancer

[36] **A'oHula** – Teaching Hula. There is no word for Choreography in Hawaiian. I suspect that has to do with Hula traditionally always being learned by watching another person dance.

can perform a solo dance. A Dancer can also pretend to be dancing with another Dancer who isn't present.

There are also Dances where there are multiple Dancers, yet none of them interact with any other Dancer. Still, most of the time, Dancers interact with at least one other Dancer. And, every Dancer might interact with every other Dancer.

Movement / Animation is often affecting multiple things at the same time. And, when Interactions are included, those affects can be interrelated between multiple things.

Summary and Communication Related Examples

My hope is that I've explained things clearly enough that you can use **Hi5ive - Aloha Edition** to enhance your Communications. You probably won't use it for small talk. You probably won't use it every day. But, when you need to really communicate about some things, when you really need to make things clear, it can really help.

I've provided some examples of how to use **Hi5ive - Aloha Edition.** However, most of those were not examples that were related to Communication. In this section I'll show you a few examples of how to use **Hi5ive - Aloha Edition** to help you communicate.

Simple and Complex Decisions

I mostly use **Hi5ive** to make certain that everybody is on the same page. I use it to make certain that everyone agrees that the correct decisions are being made with regards to a project.

Decisions are usually made with the **If** Command. They might be helped out by the **Condition** Command.

Example:

```
Condition Too-Hot
As Condition-Type=Warning
Options
Evaluation=
   If Too-Hot.Temperature > 100
      Then Too-Hot = True
   End-If
   If Too-Hot.Warning-Already-Issued = False Then
      Perform Issue-Warning
      End-Perform
   End-If
End-Condition
Copy 110
   To Too-Hot.Temperature
End-Copy
If Too-Hot
  Then
    Copy On
      To Air-Conditioning-Control
    End-Copy
  Else
    Copy Off
      To Air-Conditioning-Control
    End-Copy
End-If
```

In the above example, we turn on the A/C when the temperature get to be over 100. Until that point, perhaps we use fans instead. Hopefully, those suffice. While we're waiting until we can turn on the A/C, we wish that whoever had come up with and/or approved this logic had been a little more lenient.

We can shorten that example. We didn't have to use **Condition.** But, I wanted to show you how to do that.

There's not much ambiguity in that example. Either it's too hot or it isn't. The A/C is either on or off.

Example:

If Table-Person.Rank = King or Queen or Prince or Princess
    Then Table-Person.Rank-Type = Royalty
    Else
If Table-Person.Rank = Duke or Duchess or Marquess or Marchioness or Earl or Viscount or Viscountess or Baron or Baroness
    Then Table-Person.Rank-Type = British-Nobility
    Else
If Table-Person-Rank = Admiral or Vice Admiral or Rear Admiral or Commodore or Captain or Lieutenant Commander or Commander or Lieutenant or Midshipman
    Then Table-Person.Rank-Type = British-Navy
    Else
If Table-Person.Rank = Bishop or Priest or Deacon
    Then Table-Person.Rank-Type = Anglican-Clergy
End-If
End-If
End-If
End-If

This example figures out a person's **Rank-Type** based on their **Rank**. I could have extended the logic to include more **Rank-Types.** I could have made the **Rank-Types** less specific.

If you had a real situation like this, you might set up a table that contained every **Rank** and it's **Rank-Type.** Then, you could reduce this example as below. However, that wouldn't be as clear for discussing the details of this logic.

The previous example also illustrates an alternate indentation style for **If** that you might want to use.

```
Copy Table-Rank.Rank-Type
   To Table-Person. Rank-Type
   Through Table-Rank.Rank = Table-Person.Rank
End-Copy
```

This example matches **Table-Rank** and **Table-Person** on **Rank.** Every time there's a match, **Rank-Type** is copied from **Table-Rank** to **Table-Person.**

I worked on one project where there were a couple of very complex logic scenarios. Both of these scenarios required hierarchical decisions.

There was a main Table that had a value. There were also three helper Tables that might have a value that was of interest. Depending on that first value, one or more of those helper Tables was read based on another value in that main Table. Based on the value(s) that were retrieved you had to determine a value in the result Table.

The possible values that could be returned were assigned a number. That number indicated whether they were the first, second, third, etc., choice. Sometimes, no value was returned from the helper Tables. Then, the result value was the lowest ranking possible result value.

Some of the possible result values ranked between possible returned values. There was no direct match. When this happened, if the highest ranking helper Table value existed, but was lower than the ranking of the result value, that result value would be used.

There was slightly more to the logic than that. But, I don't remember it at this time.

As you can see, logic can get very complex, very quickly. And, when it's that complex, you need to be able to explain it to people who can understand it and verify it. **Hi5ive - Aloha Edition** makes that simpler. Still, if the logic gets to be this complex, a Diagram might work better. Using both might be your best bet.

My solution for that challenge was to create a process that would copy a few columns from the main Table into a new Table. Those columns were the ID, the value that was the first decision-maker and the values that I would enable me to pull the correct information from those helper Tables.

I then created a second process to copy all of the corresponding values from the helper Tables into that new Table.

I created a new Table of the possible result values and their ranks.

My final process went through each row of this new Table, figuring out the result value.

Others were then able to take this new Table and immediately find out what the result value would be. They didn't have to go through that uber-complex logic.

To me, the logic wasn't that complex. Well, it wasn't that complex once I broke it down. Then, I could explain it to the top-level user who let me know the result value for each and every situation. Luckily, it all boiled down to about 20 to 30 situations.

What's an Elephant?

A popular Communication Example tells about how six blind men[37] describe an Elephant. This example doesn't tell the entire story. It only tells about what these men could tell by touching the Elephant.[38]

That story makes it seem like the Elephant is just standing there not interacting with these men. But, Elephants are very social creatures. I'm sure that these men experienced much more than touching some part of the Elephant.

For one thing, the Elephant probably would have trumpeted. And, all five men would have had that experience in common. Though, the man nearest the Elephant's mouth would have had the most intense experience of that blast.

Let me give you an example in **Hi5ive - Aloha Language** that describes these men's experience the way the story does. That will keep things simple.

```
Define Elephant
   As Animal
End-Define
Element Experience
   As Text
End-Element
Element Based-On
   As Text
End-Element
```

---

[37] **Six Blind Men:** In the version I heard, there was no sixth blind man. There were only the first five.

[38] **What's an Elephant?** The PeaceCorps posts another version of this story. The blind men theorize about what an Elephant is based on what they've heard about Elephants.

```
Array Blind-Men-Experience
   Parts Experience, Based-On
End-Array
Copy The Elephant is a Pillar
   To Experience[1]
End-Copy
Copy Leg
   To Based-On[1]
End-Copy
Copy The Elephant is a Rope
   To Experience[2]
End-Copy
Copy Tail
   To Based-On[2]
End-Copy
Copy The Elephant is a Tree Branch
   To Experience[3]
End-Copy
Copy Trunk
   To Based-On[3]
End-Copy
Copy The Elephant is a Large Fan
   To Experience[4]
End-Copy
Copy Ear
   To Based-On[4]
End-Copy
Copy The Elephant is a Huge Wall
   To Experience[5]
End-Copy
Copy Belly
   To Based-On[5]
End-Copy
Copy The Elephant is a Solid Pipe
   To Experience[6]
End-Copy
Copy Tusk
   To Based-On[6]
End-Copy
Perform Connect-Animal-Parts
   Using Elephant, Blind-Men-Experience
```

Looping Blind-Men-Experience.Index from 1 by 1 until Blind-Men-Experience.Index > 6
End-Perform

We copy what each man experienced into an Array. We then use the **Connect-Animal-Parts** Routine to Combine each row of the Array into **Elephant.** Let's just assume that that Routine exists and that it combines these parts of the Elephant in the manner that you intend. If you're sharing this example with others, you might have to write out that Routine or at least explain how it works.

Often, you will want to string things together. You can create a Routine to do that and assume that everybody understands what that Routine does. **Hi5ive - Aloha Edition** provides the **Connect** Routine to do this. See Appendix E: Hi5ive Aloha Edition Comparison chapter Math and Logical Operators for more information.

We could streamline this example by replacing all of the **Copy** Commands with one instance of the version of the **Copy** Command that's in the **HanaHou HalePookay.** See the Do It Again! Chapter in the Exploring Complex Communication section for more information.

You can tell that this example is mostly for fun. That's because an Elephant is much more than the sum [connection] of their parts.

Making Reference

You might be creating a presentation, documenting a process, creating something new. Perhaps, some of your Communication has to do with Referencing something else.

You're probably Referencing other Documentation. That Documentation might be stored on a website.

You might be Referencing Theories or quoting Authorities.

You might be comparing what you're doing to what others have done, are trying to do, or are doing.

You might consider your Communication to be unique. But, most Communication is built on other Communication. And, I think that all Communication is part of some larger Communication. However, that larger Communication is much clearer than how we perceive our small part.

Example:

Let's look at making References. How would you do that in **Hi5ive - Aloha Edition?** Here's one way:

Array Location-Array
End-Array
Array File-Array
End-Array
Template First-Impression-Story
<u>Parts</u> We're building the greatest thing since sliced bread.$Reference1$ At first, it looked like $Image1$. Now, it looks like $Image2$. And, it's even better when it's toasted!$Reference2$
End-Template
Copy https://SomeWebsite.com
<u>To</u> Location-Array[1]
End-Copy

```
Copy https://SomeOtherWebsite.com
   To Location-Array[2]
End-Copy
Copy file://This PC/Pictures
   To Location-Array[2]
End-Copy
Copy Greatest-Thin-Since-Sliced-Bread-Quote.html
   To File-Array[1]
End-Copy
Copy Lumpy-Slice-Of-Bread.png
   To File-Array[2]
End-Copy
Copy Exquisite-Slice-Of-Bread.png
   To File-Array[3]
End-Copy
Copy Advantages-Of-Toasted-Bread.html
   To File-Array[4]
End-Copy
Copy Something
   To Somewhere
   Through Connect(First-Impression-
Story.$Reference1$,1Slash,Location-Array[1],File-
Array[1])
End-Copy
Copy Something
   To Somewhere
   Through Connect(First-Impression-
Story.$Image1$,1Slash,Location-Array[3],File-
Array[2])
End-Copy
Copy Something
   To Somewhere
   Through Connect(First-Impression-
Story.$Image2$,1Slash,Location-Array[3],File-
Array[3])
End-Copy
```

```
Copy Something
   To Somewhere
   Through Connect(First-Impression-
Story.$Reference2$,1Slash,Location-Array[2],File-
Array[4])
End-Copy
Copy Footnote
   To First-Impression-Story.$Reference1$.Show-As
End-Copy
Copy Image
   To First-Impression-Story.$Image1$.Show-As
End-Copy
Copy Image
   To First-Impression-Story.$Image2$.Show-As
End-Copy
Copy Footnote
   To First-Impression-Story.$Reference2$.Show-As
End-Copy
Copy First-Impression-Story
   To Printer
End-Copy
```

I specified **Something** and **Somewhere** because the **Connect** Routine does everything. **Somewhere** is the first Parameter. The **Somethings** are the location and file occurrence. The Location and File are connected with one slash.

Typically, you would use the **Constraints** attribute of the **Template** Command to point to those Locations and Files. To do that in this Example, I would have had to combine each Location and corresponding File into one thing that I could point to in **Constraints**.

The **Show-As** Property indicates how to show the References and Images. In this case, the References are shown as Footnotes. And, the Images are shown as Images.

Let's assume that **Footnote** and **Image** refer to Routines **Show-As-Footnote** and **Show-As-Image.** Those Routines somehow know what to do.

Remember, the point is to explain how something is done. We can leave out some details so long as everything is clear to ourselves and our audience.

Hi5ive – Aloha Edition Reference

This section covers various aspects and features of Hi5ive – Aloha Edition.

While I was designing **Hi5ive - Original Edition,** I started to realize that it had more usefulness than just being an App Building Language. This App Building Language could be used to clarify logic, especially between those who build Apps and speak that language and those who do not.

Years passed. Then, I decided to see if I could make **Hi5ive - Original Edition** easier to use. This version became **Hi5ive - Aloha Edition.**

First, I copied the Commands in the **Original Edition** to the **Aloha Edition.** Then, I added more Commands. These new Commands were all based on existing Commands. Yet, having them more readily available made **Hi5ive** easier to use.

While I was adding those Commands, I also saw that the **Aloha Edition** could be used to keep Communication consistent. It could be used to help people break down and simplify Communication so that everyone is able to understand it. At the same time, it would not simplify **Hi5ive** so much that it would prove clunky when used for Communication, as the **Original Edition** might have done.

Command Format

Each Command in **Hi5ive - Original Edition** consists of the same four parts, some of which are optional. In the **Aloha Edition**, that basic Command format still holds. However, there's more flexibility to it.

The basic format in the **Aloha Edition** is:

- Each Command begins with the Command and ends with **End-***Command*. So, **Comment** begins with **Comment** and ends with **End-Comment.**
- The basic appearance of a Command is best illustrated by the **Copy** and **Define** Commands. You can see how they're similar, yet slightly different.

```
Copy Calculation
  To Result
  Through Transformation
End-Copy
```

```
Define Object-Name
  As Object-Type=Object-Type
  Options Options
End-Define
```

A Command starts with the Command-Name: **Copy** / **Define** / etc.

Next, is the origin of the information or the name of something being defined. **Calculation** / **Object-Name**

Next, is a keyword or attribute prompt. This word makes the Command more readable. To / As

Next, is the result or type of object being defined. **Result** / **Object-Type=**

Next, is another keyword to make the Command readable. This last keyword and the options that follow it are usually optional. Through / Options

Next, is the information for that Keyword. **Transformation** / **Options**

The Command is ended with **End-***Command*. **End-Copy** / **End-Define**

The **bolding** in these Commands is only for clarity. The **bolding** is done automatically by **TalkStory.** [See the Aloha Edition Enhancements chapter in the Introduction section at the top of this book for more information on **TalkStory.**]

The underlining is also for clarity. It is also done automatically by **TalkStory.** The underscored parts of a Command and the part that follows it are optional. Nevertheless, in some cases, it makes no sense for a particular part of a Command to be omitted.

Take **Copy** for instance.

Example #1

Copy A
End-Copy

This example makes no sense. Where are you copying **A** to?

Example #2

Copy A
  To B
End-Copy

This example does make sense.

Actually, Example #1 can make sense if there is some default result location like a **Clipboard**. Then, Example #1 is the same as

Copy A
  To Clipboard
End-Copy.

Still, Example #1 might look erroneous. So, it's better to also specify **To**.

Let's rewrite Example #1 with the **MoveFrom** Command.

MoveFrom A
End-MoveFrom

This kind of makes sense. The default location could be **Nowhere.** In other words, we're deleting **A.** Nevertheless, let's provide some more clarity using MoveFrom in Example #2.

MoveFrom A
  To Nowhere
End-MoveFrom

I've noted those portions of each Command which are truly optional as **[Optional]** in the Command-Specific Reference section below.

End-*Command*

Each Command in **Hi5ive - Aloha Edition** is ended with **End-*Command*.** So, **If** is ended by **End-If. If** is the most important Command to end with **End-*Command*.**

Including **End-*Command*,** tells everybody exactly where each Command ends. For simple logic, this could be omitted. For more complex logic it is necessary. **End-*Command*** has been retained for clarity for all Commands everywhere in **Hi5ive - Aloha Edition,** even when the logic is simple.

This helps people avoid the tendency to omit **End-*Command*** in complex logic. Omitting **End-*Command*** can make the complex logic parts unclear. And, that's especially important with respect to the **If** Command.

Including **End-*Command*** is equally important when you're nesting Commands, one inside another. This happens when the outer Command is **Command, Routine, Perform,** or Commands like **Perform.** [See Perform, Start, Stop in the next section.]

Including **End-*Command*** is especially important when nesting the same Command inside itself.

Let's look at an example of nesting Commands:

```
Perform ...
   If ...
   Then
      Copy ...
      End-Copy
   End-If
   Perform ...
   End-Perform
End-Perform
```

We can clarify that more by adding levels to the **Perform** Command. Levels can be added to Command.

```
Perform.Level1 ...
   ...
   Perform.Level2 ...
   End-Perform.Level2
End-Perform.Level1
```

Keeping Things Clear

One way in which **Hi5ive - Aloha Edition** keeps / makes things clear, is that it vertically aligns Commands and parts of Commands. Notice the vertical alignment below.

That vertical alignment is done automatically by **TalkStory.** But, you can override it.

```
[Command - Creates a new Command.]
Command New-Command
   Is New-Command
   Does Routine
End-Command
```

Command and the corresponding **End-*Command*** are both **bolded.** Keywords starting other parts of a Command are underscored.

. (period) and **-** (hyphen / dash) are used to indicate that what comes before and after that punctuation are connected.

A period is used when the after-piece is part of the before-piece. Like **HakaPookay.Pookay.Command.**

I use a hyphen when both pieces are parts of a name. Like Person-Name. Since you create those names, you can format that however you want. You can use periods, rather than hyphens. I don't do that in order to can keep things clear.

Things in **Hi5ive - Aloha Edition** can belong to something. And, they often belong to some thing*s* [plural]. Let's take the Element Person-Name for instance:

- Person-Name can be part of a Structure as in Person-Structure.Person-Name.

- **Person-Name** is also part of the Routine in which it is defined. **Person-Routine.Person-Name.**
- Since a **Pookay** is really a large Routine, **Person-Name** is also part of the **Pookay** in which it is defined. Person in Hawaiian is Kanaka [the a's are pronounced as short *a's*]. If our **Pookay** is **Kanaka,** we could say **Kanaka.**Person-Routine.Person-Name.

Kanaka. Person-Routine. and **Person-Routine.** tell us where **Person-Name** was defined. And, that might be useful.

When **Kanaka.**Person-Routine. and **Person-Routine.** are omitted, we know that **Person-Name** was only defined once in this **Pookay.** We also know that we are referring to that definition, rather than to a **Person-Name** which is part of the definition of a Structure or some other Group.

Clarification Words

Performing **Do-Nothing** is another way to keep things clear. **Do-Nothing** is most often performed in the **If** Command. Sometimes, you want to do nothing after <u>Then</u>. Sometimes, you want to do nothing after <u>Else</u>.

```
If A=B
  Then
     Perform Do-Nothing
     End-Perform
  Else
     Copy A+B
       To C
     End-Copy
   End-If
End-If
```

<==>

Nowhere can be specified in **Copy** and Commands like **Copy**. Mostly, it is used with **MoveFrom** when you don't want to move something to something else. You just want to delete it.

```
MoveFrom File-A.Column-B
  To Nowhere
End-MoveFrom
```

<==>

All and **Any** are also clarification words. Specify **Any** or **All** for consistency and clarification, if you want to.

As clarification words **All** and **Any** mean the same thing. Use them when some Condition such as **Screen-Size** doesn't apply. You could omit **Screen-Size=Any**. If **Screen-Size** isn't specified then it's not important in this situation. Any and All Screen Sizes will be affected.

<==>

We might want any value, doesn't matter which one, out of an Array. In that case we would not say **Any**. We would say:

```
Copy Array-A.Length
  To J
  Through Random-Routine
End-Copy

Copy Array-A[J]
  To C
End-Copy
```

The first **Copy** Command passes the length of **Array-A** to **Random-Routine.** Say there are 15 Elements / values in **Array-A. Random-Routine** generates a Random Number between 1 and 15 and copies it to **J**.

The second **Copy** Command moves that Random Element of **Array-A** that is specified by **J** to **C.**

ShakaBoard

Even though there aren't that many Commands in **Hi5ive - Aloha Edition**, you might not use all of them. The **ShakaBoard** [concept] highlights those that you use most often.

Alternately, you can decide which Commands you want highlighted. You might have your reasons for highlighting some Commands that you don't use very often. You might have your reasons for not highlighting some Commands that you use frequently.

Hi5ive - Aloha Edition lets you assign Emojis to your new Commands. Hopefully, you will keep those Emojis unique and fairly easy to distinguish from Emojis for other Commands. The Emoji associated with each existing Command in the **Aloha Edition** is listed in the Command-Specific Reference Section below.

You can also assign Colors to your new Commands. However, the Colors of new Commands are usually the Color of the original **Hi5ive - Aloha Edition** Command that your Command is based on. Still, you don't have to follow that pattern. The Color associated with each existing Command in the **Aloha Edition** is listed in the Command-Specific Reference Section below.

You can change the Color that represents any Command. Just keep in mind that some people may not be able to see or perhaps distinguish that color.

You can also change the associated Emoji. However, changing Emojis and/or Colors might confuse those who are already familiar with **Hi5ive - Aloha Edition** Commands being associated with different Emojis and Colors.

In an ideal World, each user would be able to see their own version of the **ShakaBoard.** And, they would be able to override that Emoji and Color scheme to whatever suited them. That could be useful when they can't see a particular Color. That could also, as previously stated, be confusing, especially if they're trying to tell someone else what an Emoji or a Color is for a particular Command.

I've been there. Ideally, both of you do what you can to communicate clearly.

Adding new Commands allows you to use **Hi5ive - Aloha Edition** for something other than building **Pookay** and Apps. Perhaps you want to use it for Music. Your Commands would be those which help you play Music. Perhaps, **Transpose** would be one of those Commands. **Play** might be another.

These new Commands would follow the general format for all Commands in **Hi5ive - Aloha Edition**. [See The Do It Again! chapter in the Exploring Complex Communication section if you need to use a slightly different format of a Command for some reason.]

The **ShakaBoard** is also where you can find help. As you add Commands, you'll want to add help information for those Commands to the **ShakaBoard.** You can also add help information to the help information that the ShakaBoard already has for existing Commands.

Help information on the **ShakaBoard** doesn't need to be limited to **Hi5ive - Aloha Edition** commands. You can add any kind of information that will be helpful.

FAQs [Frequently Asked Questions] are often shared on websites. I place answers on my websites to questions that I think people will probably ask me. I do this in order to preempt everybody from asking me the same question. Yet, in reality, when I place that answer on my website, nobody has asked me that question, other than, perhaps, myself.

Still, I don't want to preempt people from asking me questions if they have read my FAQ's and still have questions. So, maybe I should say something like, *If I've failed to answer your question, please contact me.*

I'm fairly certain that I'm not the only person who creates FAQ for questions that they haven't been asked. I'm also certain that I'm not the only person who rarely updates their FAQs with questions that have really been asked.

The **ShakaBoard** allows you to cut and paste Commands from the **ShakaBoard** into your **Pookay.** Alternatively, you can type the name of the Command into your **Pookay.** Either way, **TalkStory** will complete the Command Format for you. This means that you don't have to remember the format for every Command, even though they're all similar and therefore not that hard to memorize.

You can use the **Copy** and **MoveFrom** Commands to copy things to and from the **ShakaBoard.** The following example copies the Help Information for the **Copy** Command from the **ShakaBoard** to the screen. [The **ShakaBoard** doesn't have to currently be showing that Help Information.]

```
Copy ShakaBoard.Help.Move
  To Screen
End-Copy
```

Aloha Edition Commands

If you have trouble locating the format or an example of a Command:

- Look at the Command-Specific Reference section. [It follows this section.]
- Look in the Index of Aloha Edition Commands. [It follows the Command-Specific Reference section.]

Below, the **Hi5ive - Original Edition** Commands are in the left-most column. [In the case of **Copy,** this is the new Command name in the **Aloha Edition.** It used to be called **Move.**]

The columns to the right of that first column contain the new **Aloha Edition** Commands that are like and based on that **Hi5ive** Command. For instance, **Element** is like and based on **Define.**

Original Edition	Aloha Edition		
Command			
Comment			
Copy	Draw	MoveFrom	Reset
	Set		
Define	Condition	Element	Feature
	File	Location	Segment
	Style	Synonym	
Group	Array	Folder	Key
	Layout	Shape	Structure
	Template	Theme	
If			
Perform	Start	Stop	
Person	Role		
Routine			

Define vs **Group**

Define Object-Name
  As Object-Type=Object-Type
  Options Options [Optional]
End-Define

[**Group** - Group things.]
Group Group-Name
  Parts Parts
  Constraints Constraints [Optional]
End-Group

Below, the Commands like **Define** are listed below **Define**. The Commands like **Group** are listed below [and to the right of] **Group**.

Groups can contain any type of Defined-Object and/or Group. Below, we see that Arrays, Keys, Layouts, Structures, and Templates typically contain Elements. Layouts typically contain Features.

Any Defined-Objects or Group can be referenced in **Options** of any Defined-Object or in **Relationships** of any Group. For instance, Styles are often referenced in Features.

Define	Group			
Condition				
Element	Array	Key	Layout	Structure
	Template			
Feature	Layout			
File	Folder			
Segment	Shape			
Location				
Style	Theme			

Layout vs **Structure** vs **Template**

Layouts position various Defined-Objects and/or Groups on a Screen, Report, or other type of Presentation. If a Screen Area is too skinny, text can wrap onto multiple lines. If a Screen Area is too small, text can become scrollable.

<==>

Structures line up Elements in Files. If text is too long to fit in an Element, it is truncated.

<==>

Templates are used with the Through part of Copy.

```
Template Template-Full-Name
  Parts $First-Name$ $Last-Name$
End-Template

Copy Structure-A
  To Element-B
  Through Template-C.$First-Name$=Structure-A.First-Name, Template-C.$Last-Name$=Structure-A.Last-Name
End-Copy
```

This Command copies the Elements **First-Name** and **Last-Name** from **Structure-A** through **Template-C** into **Element-B**.

If **Structure-A.First-Name=John** and **Structure-A.Last-Name=Doe, Element-B=Name: John Doe.**

If we moved those columns to a Structure we would get
Name: John   Doe

Or, perhaps,
John   Doe

<==>

Elements in Layouts, Structures, and Templates have the following attributes:

Mask: Can format Phone-Number, etc. For instance, **Phone-Number.Mask=(###)-###-####**. So, 360-123-9999 would become (360)-123-9999.

Default-Value: This is the default or initial value.

Prompt-Value: Only applies to Layout Elements and possibly to Template Elements. **Prompt-Value** is the value that is initially displayed to give the person who is entering that value an idea of what to enter. **Phone-Number.Prompt-Value=Enter your phone number.**

Hide-Type: Specifies how to hide Elements. **Password.Hide-Type=Password-Protect** hides the password with *…*. **Name-Hide-Type=Show** does not hide the Name. **Discount-Code.Hide-Type=Hide** hides the discount code.

Structures can be copied to Files through the **Copy** Command.

```
Copy Structure-A
  To File-A
  Through Next-Record
End-Copy
```

File vs **Folder** vs **Location**

Location defines a Location where Files and Folders exist. **File** and **Folder** can refer to that Location in the <u>Options</u> or <u>Constraints</u> part.

Tables can be treated like, and are really, Files. So, Tables have the same relationships to Folders and Locations as a File would.

Future Changes to Hi5ive

I used to say that both Editions of **Hi5ive** are Pseudo- or Meta- Languages.[39] That's not quite the case. They are rather Languages for assisting Communication. You don't need to translate your entire Communication into **Hi5ive.** Rather, you can use **Hi5ive** to help you dive deeper or clarify certain parts of your Communication.

Hi5ive - Aloha Edition allows you to add additional Commands for increased functionality. Yet, it's probably better to design an external Bookshelf of Routines (**HakaPookay**) that would provide that functionality.

At the same time, if you're going to use both **Hi5ive - Aloha Edition** and your great **HakaPookay** intensively for a certain project, you might want to merge the two for that purpose into a new Language. Still, I would keep the number of Commands to a minimum.

Hi5ive - Aloha Edition could be developed into a functioning Computer-based Language that would work similarly to an App Building Language. That could be done, if one knew how to do that and was so inclined.

Another way in which **Hi5ive - Aloha Edition** could Evolve is that it could become more globally viable. When I wrote the **Original Edition,** I looked at how Commands are stated in various App Building Languages.

If is almost always stated as **If.**

[39] **Pseudo-, Meta-, and Constructed Languages including Esperanto:** https://en.wikipedia.org/wiki/List_of_constructed_languages

Perform, on the other hand, is usually **For** or **While. For** and **While** indicate a timeframe. I preferred something that indicated that something was being done. So, I went back to the most English-Like App Building Language that I know of [**COBOL**] and used it's looping Command: **Perform.**

In went through each common Command in several App Building Languages and came up with Command Names that clearly stated what each Command did.

To make **Hi5ive - Aloha Edition** more globally viable, someone could add translation functionality to the design of **Hi5ive - Aloha Edition,** the **ShakaBoard, and TalkStory.** Then, everybody could state the Commands in their own Language.

Translation should, of course, include more than just the Command Names. There are all the Pookay, HakaPookay, and HalePookay. And, there are many other things to translate. If you do a great job at the translation, you won't just translate one word into another. You might replace entire phrases with ones that make more sense in that culture.

Of course, where **Hi5ive - Aloha Edition** goes from here depends on what you use it for and where you take it. It might also depend on if I see ways to improve it.

Who knows? I might move again. And, then, I might come up with **Hi5ive - Bali Edition.** Or, perhaps, I'll use the Ojibwe greeting and call it **Hi5ive - Boozhoo Edition.**

Command-Specific Reference

This section contains the syntax of each and every Command in **Hi5ive - Aloha Edition.** This section also contains Examples for each Command. And, there's some helpful information in regard to various Commands in this section.

The Commands are presented in the alphabetic order of the Main Commands. Commands that are like the Main Commands are listed in the same chapter as those Main Commands. The Commands are:

- **Command**
- **Comment**
- **Copy** – Commands Like **Copy:**
    - **Draw, MoveFrom, Reset, Set**
- **Define** – Commands Like **Define:**
    - **Condition, Element, Feature, File, Location, Segment, Style, Synonym**
- **Group** – Commands Like **Group:**
    - **Array, Folder, Key, Layout, Shape, Structure, Template, and Theme**
- **If**
- **Perform** – Commands Like **Perform:**
    - **Start, Stop**
- **Person** – Commands Like **Person:**
    - **Role**
- **Routine**
- **Security**

At the end of each chapter in this section that starts with the Name of a Command, there is a table which specifies the Emoji for that Command. There is also a paragraph which specifies the Color for that Command.

Command

New Commands should only be created after much contemplation as to how useful and how necessary that Command will be. Will this Command only be used for a one-time need? You should also investigate *if and how* this functionality might already exist in **Hi5ive - Aloha Edition.**

There's nothing wrong with adding new Commands to the **Aloha Edition.** You just want to keep that number to a minimum. That will keep the Language simple.

Can you just create a Routine instead? Will that be as useful? You'll probably be creating a Routine for your Command to use anyway. Do you also need to create the Command?

```
[Command - Creates a new Command.]
Command Command-Name
  Is New-Command
  Does Routine
End-Command
```

Command-Name is the name of the new Command. **New-Command** is the syntax of the new Command.

In the Example below, **Triangle-Routine** is the name of the Routine you've created to carry out the Command.

Example:

```
Command Triangle
  Is
    Triangle Triangle-Name
      As Triangle-Type
      Options Options
    End-Triangle
```

<u>Does</u> Triangle-Routine (Triangle-Name, Triangle-Type, Options)
End-Command

Note: In this example, **Shape** might be used instead of creating a new Command called **Triangle.** Still, if you're creating a lot of Triangles, it might be worth it to create the **Triangle** Command.

Once you've created a Command, it's available to every Routine you write in **Hi5ive - Aloha Edition** on your Computer System. If you would like your Command incorporated within the **Aloha Edition** globally, so that anybody can use it on any Computer System, let me know and we'll see what happens.

[Of course, this is all theoretical until somebody develops the **Aloha Edition** so that it can be used on Computers. Still, keep me apprised about what you would like to see in the **Aloha Edition.** Or, rather, in the next Edition.]

The Emoji for **Command** is below:

Command	Emoji
Command	# Grid

The Color for **Command** is Black.

Comment

Comments aren't really a Command. They're just Notes.

Good App Building / Communication includes a reasonable number of somewhat clear Summary Comments. Those Comments are spread throughout a Communication at points where those Comments are helpful. Comments should be added where appropriate.

Comments might apply to a Routine, to a set of Commands, to an Element or File or something else. It can be helpful to state what the Comment applies to within the Comment.

Both Summary and Non-Summary Comments can be included with the **Comment** Command.

[Comment – A Comment.]
Comment Comment
  Importance Importance-Level [Optional]
  FileAs Documentation-Location [Optional]
End-Comment

Importance specifies the Level of Importance of this Comment. Those Levels are up to each Team.

Importance Levels might include types of Comments such as Informational, Version, Logic, etc. Informational, for example, might imply that the Importance-Level is Normal. Informational also tells us why this Comment is important / not important.

FileAs specifies where to replace or add this Comment to external program documentation. This might be the name of a Document or other type of File, plus the location within that File. The location is probably a Comment-ID.

Not every Comment is filed for external documentation.

Examples:

Comment The Draw-Box Routine draws a box
End-Comment

<==>

Comment The Draw-Box Routine draws a box
Importance Low
FileAs File=Documents/Routines/Routine Notes.docx Routine=Draw-Box Comment-ID=2
End-Comment

You can highlight a Comment. Just type it as you would want it highlighted. For example, you can italicize *draws* in the Comment below:

Comment The Draw-Box Routine *draws* a *box*
End-Comment

The Emoji for **Comment** is below:

Command	Emoji
Comment	x x x x

The Color for **Comment** is Light Gray.

Copy, Draw, MoveFrom, Reset, Set

Copy and Commands Like Copy

Copy copies data from one place, optionally transforms it, and pastes it into another place. That transformation might be a Routine, Mask, Style, Filter, etc.

Copy in **Hi5ive - Original Edition**[40] has become the following Commands in **Hi5ive - Aloha Edition: Copy, Draw, MoveFrom, Reset,** and **Set.**

Draw creates a Shape. Shapes are then copied into Layouts.
MoveFrom moves something from somewhere, possibly to somewhere else.
Reset resets a state.
Set sets a state.

```
[Copy - Copies something to somewhere.]
Copy Calculation
  To Result
  Through Transformation [Optional]
End-Copy
```

Examples:

```
Copy A
  To B
End-Copy
```

[40] **Copy** was actually called **Move** in the **Original Edition** even though it what it did was **Copy.**

<==>

```
Copy A + B
  To C
End-Copy
```

<==>

Copy the square root of A to B.

```
Copy A
  To B
  Through Square-Root
End-Copy
```

<==>

Copy **Date-A** to **Date-B.** Input format is like `20250816`. Output format is like `16/Aug/2025`. `yyyy` is a year [`2025`]. mm is the month [`08`]. `mmm` is the month abbreviation [`Aug`]. `dd` is the day [`16`]. [`16/Aug/2025` was the date when I created this example.]

```
Copy Date-A
  To Date-B
  Through Format-In=yyyymmdd Format-
Out=dd/mmm/yyyy
End-Copy
```

<==>

```
Copy A
  To B
  Through Sort
End-Copy
```

<==>

Filtering is usually accomplished by placing **Copy** within **If** or **Perform.** However, you can say things like:

```
Copy Table-In
  To Table-Out
  Through Filter-Routine
End-Copy
```

<==>

```
Copy File-A
  To Printer
End-Copy
```

Swap examples:

Swap / Switch the values of A and B.

```
Copy A
  To B
  Through Swap
End-Copy
```

<==>

Swap numeric digits in A and B. To swap alphanumeric characters, replace Digits by Characters in the following examples.

<==>

Swap digits in positions 1 and 5. 1 and 5 can both be Arrays. That allows you to swap multiple digits at once.

```
Copy A
  To B
  Through Swap(Digits,1,5)
End-Copy
```

<==>

Swap the even and odd positioned digits.

Copy A
  To B
  Through Swap(Digits,Even,Odd)
End-Copy

Draw was added to allow for more artistic expression.

Draw creates or modifies an Art-type object. **Draw** is used to create a Shape from Segments and/or Shapes.

[**Draw** - Draws a Shape.]
Draw Shape-Name
  To Segments and/or Shapes
  Through Drawing-Options [Optional]
End-Draw

Examples:

Draw Curve-A
  To Circle-A
  Through Curve-to-Circle
End-Draw

MoveFrom was added because there was no provision for deleting something in **Hi5ive - Original Edition.**

The following command copies **A** to **B.**

Copy A
  To B
End-Copy

MoveFrom on the other hand, moves **A** to **B. A** is no longer where it was, it's at **B.**

```
MoveFrom A
  To B
End-MoveFrom
```

If you want to just move the *value* of A to B, do the following:

```
Copy A
  To B
  Through Initialize-After(A)
End-Copy
```

Or use **Reset.** More on that later in this chapter.

```
Copy A
  To B
End-Copy
Reset A
  To State.Initial
End-Reset
```

The following moves the value of **A** to **B** and deletes **A.** **Nowhere** is symbolized by a Trashcan 🗑 in many Apps.

```
Copy A
  To B
End-Copy
MoveFrom A
  To Nowhere
End-MoveFrom
```

MoveFrom is sometimes called **Delete** or **Remove.** I could have also added **Add** and **Change.** [**Change** is sometimes called **Modify** or **Update**]. But, **Add** and **Change** can more easily be handled with **Copy.** So, I didn't add them. You can create **Add, Change** and **Delete** Commands if you want to.

[**MoveFrom** - Moves something from somewhere, possibly to somewhere else.]
MoveFrom Place-to-Move-From.Item-To-Be-Moved
  To Group, File / Table, Etc.
  Through Positions [Optional]
End-MoveFrom

More Examples:

MoveFrom Group-A.Element-A
  To Nowhere
End-MoveFrom

<==>

Encrypt the value of Group-A.Element-A.
Store it in Group-B.Element-B.
Initialize Group-A.Element-A.

MoveFrom Group-A.Element-A
  To Group-B.Element-B
  Through Encryption-Routine
End-MoveFrom

<==>

Delete Row #20 from Table-A.

MoveFrom Table-A.Row(20)
  To Nowhere
End-MoveFrom

Delete all rows in File-A that have Account-Status="Obsolete".

MoveFrom File-A. Rows
  To Nowhere
  Through Account-Status="Obsolete"
End-MoveFrom

Reset was added for initialization and reinitializing Defined Objects and, more importantly, Groups. **Reset** is also useful when tracking changes.

Reset is sometimes called **Initialize** or **Reinitialize** in some App Building Languages. I'm going with **Reset,** because sometimes you want to reset something to its value at a State other than its initial State.

[**Reset** - Resets something to its value at a previous State. Transformation can be a pattern, mask, security, etc.]
Reset Element, Structure, Layout, Template, Etc.
  To State.State-Type
  Through Transformation [Optional]
End-Reset

State-Type is Initial, Previous, Next, or Current. You can also define other State-Types using **Define**.

Examples:

Reset Element-A
  To State.Initial
  Through Encryption-Routine
End-Reset

<==>

Reset Element-A
  To State.Previous
End-Reset

<==>

The following Commands return **Table-B** to how it looked at its last Commit Point. Resetting a Table to a Commit Point means backing out all the changes that were made after that point.

```
Define Last-Commit-Point
   As State-Type
End-Define
Copy Row-A
   To Table-B
   Through Commit
End-Copy
Set Table-B.State
   To Last-Commit-Point
End-Set
...
Reset Table-B.State
   To Last-Commit-Point
End-Set
```

Set was added for initializing and reinitializing Defined Objects and more importantly Groups. **Set** is also useful when tracking changes.

Set is used to remember what a value was at a certain point in time. It is also used to remember what something looked like at a certain point in time. *Put this room back the way it was!*

That point in time is a logical point in time rather than an actual time. At the same time, that logical point in time might refer to a certain time or to a time interval. **Set** says, *the value was such-and-so at this State*. **Set** sets the State.

You might or might not want to set a State every time a value changes.

You might want to set a State only after certain things have occurred.

You might want to set a State every minute or so. [Use the **If** Command to find out how much time has passed. Alternately, use the <u>Looping</u> part of **Perform.**]

[**Set** - Sets something to a previous (or future) State. In other words, that something is set to the value it held when it was last at that State or to the value it is supposed to be when it reaches that State in the future. Transformation can be a pattern, mask, security, etc.]

Set Element-State, File-State / Table-State, Layout-State, Etc.
  <u>To</u> State.State-Type
  <u>Through</u> Transformation [Optional]
End-Set

Examples:

Set Element-A.State
  <u>To</u> State.Current
End-Set

The Emojis for **Copy** and Commands like **Copy** are below:

Command	Emoji
Copy	↔ Long Left-Right Arrow
Draw	🖌 Paintbrush
MoveFrom	⊗ Circled X
Reset	🙅 Person saying No with arms crossed at wrists
Set	🙆 Person saying OK

The Color for Commands like **Copy** is the same as for **Copy:** Medium Green, even though Orange Red might be more appropriate for **MoveFrom** and **Reset.**

Define, Condition, Element, Feature, File, Location, Segment, Style, Synonym

Define and Commands Like Define

Define in **Hi5ive - Original Edition** has become the following Commands in **Hi5ive - Aloha Edition: Define, Condition, Element, Feature, File, Location, Segment, Style,** and **Synonym.**

We could also create the Command **Cell** from **Define.** A Cell is a part of a column or a row. I suggest using an Array reference instead of **Cell.** For instance, use Array-A(1,1) to refer to the first cell of Array-A.

Cell has five definitions.[41] None of those definitions describe this type of cell.

[**Define** - Defines something for later use.]
Define Object-Name
  As Object-Type=Object-Type
  Options Options [Optional]
End-Define

Object-Type can be **Condition, Element, Feature, File, Location, Segment, Style,** or **Synonym.** However, since those are now Commands in **Hi5ive - Aloha Edition,** you can use those Commands to define Objects with those Object-Types.

There are more Object-Types, like **Command.** If you need one that you don't see in this book, name it and use it. Also, do me a favor and let me know. Thanks.

[41] **Cell Definition:** https://www.google.com/search?q=cell+definition

Objects can have a Data-Type like **Number, Text, Date, Time,** Etc. Data-Types are specified in **Options.** See one of the following examples.

When the **Data-Type** is **Date, Object-Name** holds only the Date. When the **Data-Type** is **Date-Time, Object-Name** holds both the Date and the Time of Day.

Date can be treated as midnight [the beginning] of a Date. In this way, **Date** can be treated as **Date-Time.**

Time refers to a certain time today.

Time-Next is the next occurrence of that time. So, if the value is 3:00pm and it's now 1:00pm, the value is 3:00pm today. If instead, it's now 4:00pm, the value is 3:00pm tomorrow.

Time-Previous is the previous occurrence of that time.

Time-Interval can have a value of seconds or years or any other measurement of time.

Examples:

Define Element-A
  As Object-Type=Element
  Options Data-Type=Numeric, Length=9, Decimal-Places=2
End-Define

<==>

Define File-B
  As Object-Type=File
  Options Filetype=Table, Access=Input, Location=Location-C
End-Define

<==>

```
Define Location-C
  As Object-Type=Location
  Options Location Type=File-Path
End-Define
```

<==>

There is already a **Style** Command.

```
Define Bold-Style-Command
  As Object-Type=Command
  Options Font-Name="Font-Name", Bold=True
End-Define
```

Condition was added to simplify **If, Theme, Perform, Start, Stop.**

[**Condition** - Defines a Condition. That Condition can be true or false. That Condition can be set to a Severity-Level - Warning, Error, Severe Error, etc. That Condition can be set to some other Condition like Boiling.]

```
Condition Condition-Name
  As Condition-Type=Condition-Type
  Options Condition-Options [Optional]
End-Condition
```

Example:

```
Condition Too-Hot
As Condition-Type=Warning
Options
Evaluation=
   If Too-Hot.Temperature > 100
      Then Too-Hot = True
   End-If
   If Too-Hot.Warning-Already-Issued = False Then
      Perform Issue-Warning
      End-Perform
   End-If
```

End-Condition

When I was adding Commands like **Define**, I started with **Element.** I did that because Element is the basic, simplest thing to define. And, that made it easier to see how to add more complex Commands that are like **Define.**

Now that several other Commands like **Define** have been added, I could remove **Element** and just use **Define** instead.

But, I'm leaving it as an example in case you or I decide to add more Commands like **Define.**

I'm also leaving it because Elements are what I end up defining most often.

And, I'm leaving it because I'll probably want to define something other than Elements with **Define.**

[**Element** - Defines a basic Element to contain text, number, date, or other basic values.]
Element Element-Name
  As Element-Type=Element-Type
  Options Element-Options [Optional]
End-Element

Example:

Notice that Text is now an Element-Type, rather than a Data-Type. Element-Types are Text, Number, Date, Time, and perhaps some others.

Element A
  As Element-Type=Text
End-Element

Feature was added to style websites (and other presentations).

[**Feature** - Defines a Feature of a Theme. Buttons, Pictures, Menus, Inputs, Outputs, Areas for Text, ...]

Feature Feature-Name
  As Feature-Type=Feature-Type
  Options Feature-Options [Optional]
End-Feature

Example:

Feature Button-A
  As Feature-Type=Button
  Options Style=Button-Style-A
End-Feature

File was added for input/output.

[**File** - Defines a File / Table. Options include the Location of the File. Options might include whether the File can only be read. Options might specify Security for the File.]

File File-Name
  As File-Type=File-Type
  Options Options [Optional]
End-File

Example:

File File-A
  As File-Type=Text-Sequential
  Options Access=Read-Only, Location=Location-A
End-File

Those who build Apps are used to using very specific File-Types like .txt [text], .docx [Microsoft Word Document], .xlsx [Microsoft Excel Spreadsheet], .html [website], etc. **Hi5ive -**

Aloha Edition can use those. It can also use more generic File-Types like **Pookay, Picture, Text, Document, Spreadsheet,** etc.

File Locations are defined with the **Location** Command below.

Location was added to specify where Files are located.

In Computer terms, a Location is a Path or a URL.
A Location can be a partial Path or a complete Path [specifying the Path, File, and File-Type], depending on what is needed.
A Location can also be more generic as in *Second Floor*.
A Location can be a set of coordinates.

In Communication terms, a Location can be vague, like:

- *Over there.*
- *Somewhere in Outer Space.*

[**Location** - Defines a Location for Files / Tables or a Folder. **Location** can use existing Locations to Define new Locations. Options can specify Security for the Location.]
Location Location-Name
  As Location-Type=Place
  Options Options [Optional]
End-Location

Examples:

Location Location-A
  As Location-Type=Stubbart.com
  Options Internet-Website [Optional]
End-Location

<==>

Location Location-B
  As Location-Type=Hi5ive - Aloha Edition
  Options Folder-Documents/Stories/Computer-Stories
End-Location

Segment was added to allow for artistic expression.

[**Segment** - Defines a line, something like a line, or a basic part of a Shape. A Segment is a simple shape like a dot, line, curve / arc, arrow, squiggle, etc. Basically, this is a 1D-Shape. Segment can be thick, thin, or in-between.]
Segment Segment-Name
  As Segment-Type=Segment-Type
  Options Options [Optional]
End-Segment

Example:

Segment Line-A
  As Segment-Type=Line
  Options Font=Font-A, Color=Blue, Background-Color=Azure Screen-Size=All
End-Segment

Style was added to style websites (and other presentations).

[**Style** - Defines a Style. Style-Type can specify what this style can be used for - Generic, Buttons, Text, Images, etc. Options include all the Style Attributes - Font Attributes, Colors - text and background, Borders, spacing, placement, etc. Options can also include the media for which the Style is valid. All-Media, Screen, Phone, Printer, etc.]
Style Style-Name
  As Style-Type=Style-Type
  Options Options [Optional]
End-Style

Example:

Style Style-A
As Style-Type=Text
Options Font=Font-A, Color=MidnightBlue, Background-Color=Azure, Media=All-Media
End-Style

Synonym was added when I realized that in some situations, names of Routines could get very long. And, it could become tedious to spell everything out every time. That could also lead to errors. **Synonym** is also useful in other situations where you need an alternate name.

[**Synonym** - Defines a Synonym. A Synonym is another (usually shorter) name for something else.]
Synonym Synonym-Name
As Synonym-Type=Synonym-Type
Options Options [Optional]
End-Synonym

Example:

Synonym Synonym-2D
As Synonym-Type=Alternate-Name
Options Reference=**HanaNo'eau.Ki'i'Ike.**
2D**Ki'i'Ike**
End-Synonym

The Emojis for **Define** and Commands like **Define** are below:

Command	Emoji
Define	🛠 Hammer and Wrench
Condition	❓ Enclosed Question Mark [Question Mark=**If**]
Element	⨀ Dot in Circle (Hydrogen – 1st Element)

Command	Emoji
Feature	🖌 Paintbrush
File	🗐 Multiple Pages
Location	⚓ Anchor
Segment	⊖ Lines and Arcs
Style	ξ Greek Letter xi
Synonym	≛ Star Equals

The Color for Commands like **Define** is the same as for **Define:** Medium Blue.

Group, Array, Folder, Key, Layout, Shape, Structure, Template, Theme

Group and Commands Like Group

A Group can be a Group of zero items.[42]

A Group can be a Group of one item.

Most Groups, however, contain multiple items. And, sometimes a Group isn't considered to be a Group if it's under a certain size or if not enough members are present. A Group also might not be considered to be a Group if it doesn't have enough structure.

Group in **Hi5ive - Original Edition** has become the following Commands in **Hi5ive - Aloha Edition: Group, Array, Folder, Key, Layout, Shape, Structure, Template,** and **Theme. Group** can also be a column / field, a row / record, or an entire Table/File.

Items in various columns of an Array have the same Object-Type. For instance, Column-A might contain numbers. Column-B might contain text.

That might also occur in a Structure. A Structure can be defined to contain multiple Structures. So, using the first Structure, you might have a column like you would in an Array for several rows. And, then, using the second Structure, you might have something else for several rows where that column previously existed.

A File / Table might contain two Structures: One for summary information and one for detailed information. Or, the second sub-

[42] **A Group of Zero Items** is sometimes called a Null Group. This is like an egg carton with no eggs in it.

Structure might contain transactional data and the first might contain things like name and address.

Those two Structures don't need to line up anywhere. That is, columns in one Structure can overlap columns in the other. And, multiple columns in one Structure use the space of one column in the other Structure.

```
[Group - Group things.]
Group Group-Name
  Parts Parts
  Constraints Constraints [Optional]
End-Group
```

Examples:

```
Group Array-A
  Parts A
  Constraints Index=I-Index, Occurs=100
End-Group

<==>

Group Structure-C
  Parts A, B
  Constraints A.Index=I-Index, A.Occurs=100
End-Group
```

Array was added because Arrays are usually a basic group in App Building Languages. Arrays can take advantage of looping in the **Perform** Command. And, you can easily point to any part of the Array, if you know where that part is.

An Array is a Group that is made of one or more columns.

Each part of a column in an Array represents some value for a Defined-Object or Group. Arrays usually contain Elements. But, they can just as easily contain Conditions, Structures, etc.

A limit is the maximum number of occurrences / values that an Array can have.

Arrays might be sorted.

[**Array** -a list of items. Each item can be accessed by an index / subscript. A(1) and A(first) refer to the first item in the list.]

Array Array-Name
Parts Elements (or other Defined-Objects or Groups)
Constraints Starting-Points, Limits, (other Constraints) [Optional]
End-Array

Examples:

Array Array-A
Parts Element-A
Constraints Start-Range=1, Limit=10
End-Array

<==>

In the following example, No limit has been set for Array-B. I don't usually define Arrays to have limits. Almost every time I do, I end up needing to up that limit.

Actually, Array-B does have a limit. It's some ridiculously high number. So, most of the time, you don't need to worry about what that is. I have surpassed that limit a few times. That's not normal. And, it usually means there's an error. Something went wrong.

Array Array-A-2D
Parts Array-A, Array-B
Constraints Array-A.Start-Range=1, Array-A.Limit=10, Array-B.Start-Range=0
End-Array

Folder was added to group Files. It was also added to work with entire Databases. In that case, a Folder is sometimes called a Schema.

[**Folder** - Group of Files / Tables in a Folder / Database.]
Folder Folder-Name
Parts Files (or other Defined-Objects or Groups)
Constraints Constraint-Methods (and other Constraints) [Optional]
End-Folder

Examples:

Folder Folder-A
Parts File-A, File-B, File-C
Constraints Relate-by-All-Keys
End-Folder

<==>

Folder Folder-A
Parts File-A, File-B, File-C
Constraints Layout-A
End-Folder

<==>

Folder Database-A
Parts Table-A, Table-B, Table-C
End-Folder

Key was added to speed up Files / Tables. **Key** was also added to relate Tables to other Tables.

A Key might be based on the values of certain fields / columns. I typically say *fields* when referring to Files and *columns* when referring to Tables. But, fields and columns are basically the same.

A Key might be a certain record number in the File.
Examples: First, Last, 245, -245 (counting starting with Last), Next, Next + 10, Previous, Previous - 10.

The types of Keys include: Main-Key, Alternate-Key, External-Key, Reference-Key, Sequential-Key. External Keys are actually fields in a different File / Table. Those fields might be a Key in that other File. Files might only have Reference-Keys and Sequential-Keys.

External-Keys provide a link between two Files / Tables or Groups. External-Keys ensure that the values of those Keys are kept in sync.

Reference-Keys are similar to External-Keys. However, Reference-Keys provide no guarantee that those values are in sync.

Another type of Key is Index-Key. Index-Keys often access the File / Table more quickly.

You can specify multiple types of Keys for the same Key.

For Communication, Keys are probably Search-Keys or Key-Words.

[**Key** - Defines a Key of a File / Table or any Type of Group. Files and Tables can have zero to many Keys.
Constraints specify the File / Table where this Key resides. Constraints can also specify the type of Key.]
Key Key-Name
Parts Fields / Columns (or other Defined-Objects or Groups)
Constraints File / Table (other places this Key might reside), Key-Type, (or other Constraints) [Optional]
End-Key

Example:

Key Key-A
Parts Column-A, Column-B, Column-C
Constraints File=File-A, Key-is-Indexed, Key-is-Main-Key
End-Key

Layout was added to style websites (and other presentations). A Layout is a group of Elements arranged visually.

[**Layout** - Group of Elements in a presentation layout. **Layout** is presentation layout. It is a report, screen, chart, website, etc. or a part of one of those. **Layout** can be a Database Schema that contains the relationships between the Tables.]
Layout Layout-Name
Parts Elements (or other Defined-Objects or Groups)
Constraints Conditions (or other Constraints) [Optional]
End-Layout

Example:

Layout Layout-A
Parts Header, Detail-Record-1, Detail-Record-2, Detail-Record-3, Footer
Constraints Detail-Record-2.When-Present, Detail-Record-3.When-Present, Detail-Record-3.Repeats
End-Layout

Shape was added to allow for artistic expression.

[**Shape** - Group of Segments and/or Shapes. **Shape** is a geometric shape. This can be a 2D shape - square, circle, or a more complex 2D shape. This can be a 3D shape - cube, sphere, saddle, etc.]

Shape Shape-Name
Parts Features (or other Defined-Objects or Groups)
Constraints Placement, Animation, (or other Constraints) [Optional]
End-Shape

Example:

Shape Pentagon-A
Parts Square-A, Triangle-A
Constraints Triangle-A.Placement=Square-A.Top, Triangle-A.Color=Red, Show-Connecting-Points=False
End-Shape

Structure was added to show / explain how the data is arranged in a File / Table.

Structure creates a Data-Structure. **Parts** are typically Elements. **Constraints** often tell where various Parts of the Structure start. These might overlap with other Parts.

[**Structure** - Group of Elements. **Structure** contains multiple Elements. A simple structure would contain various Elements. Structures can get much more complex.]

Structure Structure-Name
Parts Elements (or other Defined-Objects or Groups)
Constraints Starting Positions of Various Parts (or other Constraints) [Optional]
End-Structure

Example:

Structure Structure-A
  Parts Element-A, Element-B, Element-C, Element-D
  Constraints Element-A.Overlay=Element-D
End-Structure

Template was added to combine text and Elements into longer text. This is useful for presentations. **Constraints** specify the relationship between **Parts** and other Defined-Objects and/or Groups. **Constraints** might also specify things like how many spaces to leave between **Part-Names.**

Template typically trims [removes leading and trailing spaces] Elements and groups them together. You can specify a Constraint of **Trim=False.**

[**Template** - Templates are used to Group Elements together. Parts are surrounded by any special character - #, $, %, and & work well. Surrounding those Elements distinguishes them from text.]
Template Template-Name
  Parts Part-Names (or Text or other Defined-Objects or Groups)
  Constraints Relationships to other Defined-Objects or Groups (or other Constraints) [Optional]
End-Template

Example:

Part-Indicator specifies the special character(s) that indicate(s) a Part. The Default value for Part-Indicator is $, but I specify it in the example anyway. Just to be clear.

Template Template-A
  Parts A long time ago on $Date-1$ $Count-1$ funny things happened.

Constraints $Date-1$=Date-A, $Count-1$=10, Part-Indicator=$
End-Template

Elements can be copied to **Parts** using the **Copy** Command, rather than by using Constraints. You can also use both the **Copy** Command and Constraints. If Template Elements are specified in both, the Copy Command has the final say. See the Hi5ive – Aloha Edition Commands chapter above.

Try to use the same special character as the **Part-Indicator** for every Part. Make certain **Part-Indicator** is not part of the text or part of a Part-Name. If you can't find a special character that qualifies, try to use more than one special character, like ## or $$ or #$.

You *can* use multiple Part-Indicators. For example, you can use one Part-Indicator for some Parts and another for the rest. But, that becomes messy.

Theme was added to style websites (and other presentations).

[**Theme** - Group of Styles to be used in a picture or presentation.]
Theme Theme-Name
Parts Styles (or other Defined-Objects or Groups)
Constraints Conditions (or other Constraints) [Optional]
End-Theme

Example:

Theme Theme-A
Parts Style-A, Style-B
Constraints Theme-A.Style-A.Screen-Size=All
Theme-A.Style-B.Screen-Size=Screen-Size-Large
End-Theme

The Emojis for **Group** and Commands like **Group** are below:

Command	Emoji
Group	Grouped Lines
Array	4 horizontal lines
Folder	Open File Folder
Key	Key
Layout	Open newspaper
Shape	Dot within Diamond
Structure	a b c d
Template	Asterisk inside Square
Theme	Artist's Pallet

The Color for Commands like **Group** is the same as for **Group:** Light Blue.

If

[If - Does things based on a Condition. That Condition might be simple or complex.]

If Condition
  __Then__ Commands
  __Else__ Commands
End-If

If allows a Routine to perform or not perform Commands based on some Condition. **Condition** specifies the Condition when these Commands are performed.

That Condition is usually something like **A=B.** Nevertheless, it can be more complicated like **A=B and C not = D.** Parentheses are used to group Conditions as in **A=B and (C not = D or C=E).** This can eliminate ambiguity as to which Condition is tested in combination with which other Conditions(s). Conditions are evaluated in the order that they are encountered [left to right, but evaluated within parentheses first].

Conditions can also be defined with the **Condition** Command. See the Define, Condition, Element, Feature, File, Location, Segment, Style, Synonym chapter above.

When the Condition is met (true), the Commands following __Then__ are performed.

When the Condition is not met (false), the Commands following __Else__ are performed.

The __Else__ keyword and its following Commands are optional.

When __Else__ is specified, __Then__ and its following Commands are optional.

Example:

If A=B
  Then
    Copy C
      To D
    End-Copy
  Else
    Copy C
      To E
    End-Copy
End-If

The Emoji for **If** is below:

Command	Emoji
If	？Full-Width Question Mark

The Color for **If** is Medium Purple.

Perform, Start, Stop

Perform and Commands Like Perform

Additional Commands in **Hi5ive - Aloha Edition** that are like **Perform** are **Start** and **Stop.**

[**Perform** - Performs / does / executes / runs one or more Commands and/or Routines.]
Perform Command-Name(s) / Routine-Name(s)
  Using Parameters [Optional]
  Looping Conditions [Optional]
End-Perform

Perform performs Routines and/or Commands. Routines sometimes need parameters / values passed to them. Routines or Commands can be performed 0, 1, or many times, depending on the Conditions stated after Looping.

Instead of using Looping, **Perform** can be placed within **If.**

One or more of the Commands or Routines that are being performed can sometimes change the values that are associated with Looping. This causes **Perform** to quit looping at a different point than where it initially looked like it would quit looping..

Examples:

Perform Print-Routine
End-Perform

<==>

```
Perform Print-Routine
  Using File-A
End-Perform

<==>

Perform Print-Routine
  Using File-A
  Looping from 1 to 9
End-Perform

<==>

Perform Print-Routine
  Using File A
  Looping until Condition=Out-of-Paper
End-Perform
```

Perform waits until the previous Command is finished before it starts. But, what if you want two Routines to happen at the same time?[43]

Then, you would Perform the first Routine using **Wait=False** as one of the Using parameters.

---

[43] **Having two Routines that are in the same App and happen at the same time** is called Parallel Processing.

It might also be called Threading. However, Threading runs the Routine at the same time with different parameters. And, there might be timing delays between when one occurrence of the Routine starts and when the next one starts. You can use another parameter to specify that delay. **Delay-Time=Amount of Time.**

I added **Start** and **Stop** to the **Aloha Edition** when I realized that there weren't any timing Commands.

I could have added more Scheduling Commands in addition to **Start** and **Stop.** Nevertheless, I decided to keep **Hi5ive - Aloha Edition** simple and didn't.

A Scheduling **HakaPookay** can be used [or created and used] if you need more Scheduling Commands. However, Scheduling **HakaPookay** don't really do much more than **Start** and **Stop.**

Scheduling **HakaPookay** will allow you to create meetings and tasks. Those meetings and tasks can occur multiple times.

You can invite others to your meeting. You can also invite a meeting room and a meeting method – Video Conference, phone, etc.

See the Events, Their Initiators and Terminators chapter in the Exploring Basic Communication section above for more information.

You can do all of that scheduling with **Hi5ive - Aloha Edition**. Still, you might want to use a Scheduling **HakaPookay**[44] instead.

See the Going Somewhere? chapter in Appendix E: Other App Building Languages for more information on how to use **Start** and **Stop** to start and stop Commands and Routines.

[Start – Starts an Event, Command, or Routine.]

---

[44] Scheduling **HakaPookay.** I would call this **Hanana.** Hanana means Event in Hawaiian. The a's are pronounced as short *a's*.

Events are what you're probably scheduling. You might also be scheduling people. But, you're probably scheduling them in association with Events.

Start Event-Name
Using Date-Time [Optional]
Looping Start-Condition=Condition-A, Stop-After=Time-A1, Start-At=Time-A2, Stop-After=Time-B1, Stop-At=Time-B2, Stop-Condition=Condition-B, etc. [Optional]
End-Start

Example:

Start Routine-A
Using Start-At=5:00pm
End-Start

If I want **Routine-A** to start at **5:00pm** every day, I can place the **Start** Command within a **Perform** Command. If I want **Routine-A** to start this Saturday at 5:00pm, I specify **16-Aug-2025 5:00pm**.

[**Stop** - Stops an Event, Command, or Routine.]
Stop Event-Name
Using Date-Time [Optional]
Looping Stop-Condition=Condition-A, Stop-After=Time-B1, Stop-At=Time-B2, Stop-For=Time-B3 [Optional]
End-Stop

Example:

Stop Current-Routine
Looping Stop-For=Wait-Time
End-Stop

The Emojis for **Perform** and Commands like **Perform** are below:

Command	Emoji
Perform	⭯ Circle Arrow
Start	↦ Rightwards Arrow from Bar
Stop	⇥ Rightwards Arrow to Bar

The Color for Commands like **Perform** is the same as for **Perform:** Light Green, even though Tomato might be more appropriate for **Stop.**

Person, Role

Person and Commands Like Person

The additional Command in **Hi5ive - Aloha Edition** that is like **Person** is **Role.**

Person describes a Person.

A Person might be a Computer User, a Contact, or somebody else.

A Person might be a pet or some other entity that you interact with in the same way that you interact with a Person.

A Person might be an entity that you interact with in a way that is similar to the way that you interact with a Person.

These days, a Person might be an AI or Robot. But, I don't classify them as People.

```
[Person - Describes someone.]
Person Who
  Is Description [Optional]
  Attributes Attributes [Optional]
End-Person
```

Attributes can include Aliases / Nicknames / Preferred Names / Pen-Names / Stage-Names / etc.

Example:

```
Person Dale-Stubbart
  Is "The Author of Hi5ive - Aloha Edition"
  Attributes Hair-Color=Brown, Eye-Color=Hazel
End-Person
```

In **Hi5ive - Original Edition,** Roles were predefined. And, there were a limited number of them.

In the **Aloha Edition,** you can use the **Role** Command to make Roles more flexible. Predefined Generic Roles like Read-Only still exist. However, you can make things clearer by using Roles that you create yourself.

Roles are used in the **Security** Command.

[**Role** - Describes a Role.]
Role Title
  Is Description [Optional]
  Attributes Attributes [Optional]
End-Role

Example:

Role Low-Level-User
  Is given the least access
  Attributes All-Data=Read-Only-Access, Security-Data=No-Access
End-Role

Attributes specifies the data (Tables, Files, …) and what access each one gets.

If Attributes are not specified, No-Access is given.

I've been on Projects where I was not given any access. I often wish that I was given more access.

At the same time, I'm glad that my access to the Production computer environment is restricted or not available. I usually don't really need to see what's happening there. And, I *really* don't want to mess it up.

For practical reasons, **Hi5ive - Aloha Edition** comes with an All-Access Role. Otherwise, nobody could do anything.

This Role should be limited to a few people. You might also want to limit access to the **Role** Command and to various **Role.**<u>**Attributes**</u> values.

The Emojis for **Person** and Commands like **Person** are below:

Command	Emoji
Person	🧑 Person
Role	🥸 Disguised Face

The Color for Commands like **Person** is the same as for **Person**: Tan.

Routine

[**Routine** - A set of Commands. Routines can become Commands. However, the number of Commands should be limited. Otherwise, things can become complicated and that's not the purpose of any edition of **Hi5ive.**]

Routine Routine-Name
  Using Parameters
  Commands Commands
End-Routine

Routine is used to define a Routine. Parameters can be passed to and from Routines. **Parameters** are Defined-Objects and Groups.

Example:

Routine Routine-A
  Using A, B
  Commands
    Comment Routine A Copies the value of A to B and the value 5 to A
    End-Comment
    Copy A
      To B
    End-Copy
    Copy 5
      To A
    End-Copy
End-Routine

Within a Routine, you don't immediately know the Data-Types of **A** and **B**. Those were defined outside the Routine. We can, however, find out their Data-Types and other things about **A** and **B**. We can look at:

A.Data-Type
B.Parts
A.Object-Type
B.Relationships
A.Options
Etc.

It's best to look at **Object-Type** first. Based on that, you can try to look further. Everything should have a default value. For instance, Defined-Objects will have **Data-Type=Generic** if **Data-Type** is not specified in **Options.**

Lots of things, however, can be specified in **Options** and **Relationships.** So, you might find that **A.Halloween=Unknown** or **B.Christmas=Undefined.** (**Unknown** and **Undefined** mean the same thing.)

The return value of a Routine might be returned to an Element, Array, etc. The following Example shows you how to do that:

```
Perform Routine-B
  Using A,B
End-Perform
Copy Routine-B.Value
  To C
End-Copy
...
Routine Routine-B
  Using A, B
  Commands
    If B > A
      Then
        Copy False
          To Routine-B.Value
        End-Copy
    End-If
End-Routine
```

An easier way to do that is to define those variables outside of the Routine. Those variables will be available both within and outside of that Routine.

```
Define A
   As Number
End-Define
Define B
   As Number
End-Define
Define C
   As Number
End-Define
Copy 5
  To A
End-Copy
Copy 6
  To B
End-Copy
Perform Routine-C
End-Perform
...
Routine Routine-C
  Commands
    If B > A
      Then
        Copy False
           To C
        End-Copy
    End-If
End-Routine
```

The Emoji for **Routine** is below:

Command	Emoji
Routine	○ Circle

The Color for **Routine** is Dark Gray.

Security

[**Security** - Assigns people to various Security Roles and can further limit their Access within that Role.]
Security Role
<u>For</u> Subject
<u>Access</u> Object-Name, Access-Type, Level [Optional]
End-Security

Security assigns Security for an object to a subject. Like **Role,** access to **Security** and **Security.**<u>Access</u> values should be limited to a few people.

Role is defined using the **Role** Command. See the Person, Role chapter above.

Subject can be anything which is defined – a Person, File, Group, Routine, etc. It can be multiple things.

Access-Type includes **Read, Write, Insert, Change, Delete,** combinations of those, and more.

Level sets different clearance levels.

Example:

Security Read-Only-Role
<u>For</u> Dale-Stubbart
<u>Access</u> Object-Name=File-A, Access-Type=Read, Level=Top
End-Security

Since Access-Type includes Insert, Change, Delete, I might want to go back and rethink adding those Commands. However, I'm not going to do that at this time. I'm going to let circumstances determine whether something is Inserted, Changed, or Deleted.

Insert is the result of **Copy** or **MoveFrom** being able to add something to a File / Table.

Change is the result of **Copy** or **MoveFrom** modifying something in a File / Table.

Delete is **MoveFrom** removing something from a Table.

The Emoji for **Security** is below:

Command	Emoji
Security	🔒 Lock

The Color for **Security** is Dark Red.

About the Author

Hello, my name is Dale Stubbart. I live in Hawaii. I have written more than 130 books. In addition to being a Computer Consultant, I am also a Transformation Consultant. That means, I help people restore themselves and those around them to wholeness. Those around them includes spaces that they live in – their house, their yard, their vehicle.

You can find out more about my Transformation Consulting work and the help that I offer at Stubbart.com. You can also find all of my books there.

I've worked with Computers for 45 years, mostly as a Consultant. A lot of that work includes transforming computers, apps, programming languages, and data. I also build websites and help people organize their computers.

I create shortcuts in Microsoft Word and greatly speed up my editing and writing of books. I also figure out other ways to speed up computers.

Majoring in both Language and Computer Science in college came in handy when I was writing this book. As far as Languages went, I majored in Spanish and took one year of French. If I could have afforded to attend that College for a fourth year, I might have had a minor in French and a major in Modern Foreign Languages.

I've always treated Math, my third major, as a Language. You might think that's weird but it helped me ace one Math Course in College. So, you never know.

I also treat Languages as Math. This helped me instantly figure out the spelling rules for Spanish and start to aces those tests in 9th grade. Before that, I was in danger of flunking.

Hi5ive - Aloha Edition

A Simple Language for
Communicating with Deep Understanding

I got the Idea for **Hi5ive - Original Edition** from a Professor at College. He developed a functioning App Building Language using a minimum of Commands. I had graduated by the time he finished creating that Language. So, I don't know what those Commands were or how many of them he ended up with.

I took a different approach several years later to create the design of an App Building Language with a minimum number of Commands. That became **Hi5ive - Original Edition.**

Several more years later, I enhanced that design to make that Language easier to use. That included adding some Commands.

I also geared this new Language more toward Communication. There's still a minimal number of Commands in the new edition of this Language. I call it **Hi5ive - Aloha Edition.**

Of my more than 130 books, 10 are Computer Books. 20 are Earthwise Books. 10 are Transformational Books. 10 are Food, Travel, and Other Reference Books. That leaves 80 that are Fantasy, Fiction, Sci-Fi, Lite-Horror, Romance, and Children's Books.

So, even though I'm a Computer Expert, most of my books are not about Computers. I make Computer Books interesting. Still, they're not that interesting! Even so, my number 1 best selling book is <u>Consulting 101 – The Basics</u>. In it, I share about my Computer Consulting experience and what that life is like.

Whether you're heavily into Computers or not, you might find my other Computer Books to your liking.

- In Search of a Right-Brained Computer
- A Short, All Inclusive Course in Emojis
- Expressive Websites
- Fonts and Special Characters for Websites
- Hardwired: Staying Wired in a Wireless Age

Hi5ive - Aloha Edition

A Simple Language for
Communicating with Deep Understanding

- Take Control of your Internet Posts: Blog Your Own Way
- A Greener Printer
- Designing Your Website to Use Less Energy

There's also Ribo Quadrilobe: In The Healer is Judged. (Ribo is a Robot who becomes more than the sum of his parts.)

That book looks at the separation of church and state. It also has a good deal of humor and some romance. There's not that much in it about how Computers work.

You can find all of my books at Stubbart.com.

Indexes and Lists

These Indexes and Lists will help you keep track of things. They will also help you navigate your way through this book.

The Index of Aloha Edition Commands will help you find examples of each Command.

Properties lists all properties that are mentioned in this book. They help cut down on the number of **Define** Commands that you have to use. They help you reveal hidden values.

Clarification Words are really Filler Words. They help you understand what's going on. Without them, it would look like something is missing.

The Index of **Pookay, HakaPookay,** and **HalePookay** helps you find where those are mentioned and explained.

Index of Aloha Edition Commands

The Titles of sections in this book are preceded by .

The Titles of chapters are preceded by .

In print versions of this book, the Titles of sections are underlined.

The Titles of Chapters are not underlined, even in print versions of this book.

Below, you'll find each **Aloha Edition** Command and the sections and chapters that it can be found in. The Commands are listed in alphabetical order.

Command	Section	Chapter
Comment (cont.)	Command-Specific Reference	Comment
	Command-Specific Reference (cont.)	Routine
Condition	Exploring Basic Communication	Handling Errors
	Command-Specific Reference	Define, Condition, Element, Feature, File, Location, Segment, Style, Synonym
	Summary and Communication Related Examples	Simple and Complex Logic
Copy	Information Communication Examples	Information Reports and Charts
		Information Security
		Information Storage
	Exploring Basic Communication	Handling Errors
	Exploring Advanced Communication	Thoughts and Beyond
	Exploring Complex Communication	Music
		Do It Again!
	Communication Examples	What's an Elephant
	Hi5ive – Aloha Edition Reference	Command Format
		Keeping Things Clear
		ShakaBoard
		Aloha Edition Commands

Command	Section	Chapter
Copy (cont.)	Command-Specific Reference	Copy, Draw, MoveFrom, Reset, Set
		If
		Routine
	Summary and Communication Related Examples	Simple and Complex Logic
		What's an Elephant?
		Making Reference
Define	Introduction	Hi5ive – Original Edition: Quick Overview
	Information Communication Examples	[Section]
		Information Reports and Charts
	Exploring Intermediate Communication	Patterns and Pattern Recognition
	Exploring Complex Communication	Do It Again!
	Communication Examples	What's an Elephant
	Hi5ive – Aloha Edition Reference	Command Format
		Aloha Edition Commands
	Command-Specific Reference	Copy, Draw, MoveFrom, Reset, Set
		Define, Condition, Element, Feature, File, Location, Segment, Style, Synonym
		Routine

Command	Section	Chapter
Define (cont.)	Summary and Communication Related Examples	What's an Elephant?
Draw	Command-Specific Reference	Copy, Draw, MoveFrom, Reset, Set
Element	Introduction	More on Pookay and HakaPookay
	Communication Examples	What's an Elephant?
	Command-Specific Reference	Define, Condition, Element, Feature, File, Location, Segment, Style, Synonym
	Summary and Communication Related Examples	What's an Elephant?
Feature	Command-Specific Reference	Define, Condition, Element, Feature, File, Location, Segment, Style, Synonym
File	Introduction	Hi5ive – Original Edition: Quick Overview
		Aloha Edition Enhancements
		More on Pookay and HakaPookay
	Information Communication Examples	Information Reports and Charts
		Information Security

Command	Section	Chapter
File (cont.)	Command-Specific Reference	Define, Condition, Element, Feature, File, Location, Segment, Style, Synonym
Folder	Command-Specific Reference	Group, Array, Folder, Key, Layout, Shape, Structure, Template, Theme
Group	Exploring Intermediate Communication	Naming Conventions
	Exploring Complex Communication	Do It Again!
	Hi5ive – Aloha Edition Reference	Aloha Edition Commands
	Command-Specific Reference	Group, Array, Folder, Key, Layout, Shape, Structure, Template, Theme
If	Information Communication Examples	Information Reports and Charts
	Exploring Basic Communication	Handling Errors
	Exploring Intermediate Communication	Patterns and Pattern Recognition
	Exploring Advanced Communication	Thoughts and Beyond
	Hi5ive – Aloha Edition Reference	Keeping Things Clear
	Command-Specific Reference	Define, Condition, Element, Feature, File, Location, Segment, Style, Synonym
		If

Command	Section	Chapter
If (cont.)	Command-Specific Reference	Routine
	Summary and Communication Related Examples	Simple and Complex Logic
Key	Command-Specific Reference	Group, Array, Folder, Key, Layout, Shape, Structure, Template, Theme
Layout	Information Communication Examples	Information Reports and Charts
	Command-Specific Reference	Group, Array, Folder, Key, Layout, Shape, Structure, Template, Theme
Location	Information Communication Examples	Information Security
	Command-Specific Reference	Define, Condition, Element, Feature, File, Location, Segment, Style, Synonym
MoveFrom	Introduction	Let's Start with an Example
	Hi5ive – Aloha Edition Reference	Command Format
		Keeping Things Clear
	Command-Specific Reference	Copy, Draw, MoveFrom, Reset, Set
Perform	Information Communication Examples	Information Reports and Charts

Command	Section	Chapter
Perform (cont.)	Exploring Basic Communication	Handling Errors
	Communication Examples	What's an Elephant?
	Hi5ive – Aloha Edition Reference	Command Format
	Command-Specific Reference	Define, Condition, Element, Feature, File, Location, Segment, Style, Synonym
		Perform, Start, Stop
		Routine
	Summary and Communication Related Examples	What's an Elephant?
Person	Information Communication Examples	Information Security
	Exploring Intermediate Communication	Naming Conventions
	Command-Specific Reference	Person, Role
Reset	Information Communication Examples	Information Reports and Charts
	Command-Specific Reference	Copy, Draw, MoveFrom, Reset, Set
Role	Information Communication Examples	Information Security
	Command-Specific Reference	Person, Role

Command	Section	Chapter
Routine	Information Communication Examples	Information Reports and Charts
	Command-Specific Reference	Routine
Security	Information Communication Examples	Information Security
	Command-Specific Reference	Security
Segment	Command-Specific Reference	Define, Condition, Element, Feature, File, Location, Segment, Style, Synonym
Set	Command-Specific Reference	Copy, Draw, MoveFrom, Reset, Set
Shape	Command-Specific Reference	Group, Array, Folder, Key, Layout, Shape, Structure, Template, Theme
Start	Exploring Basic Communication	Events, Their Initiators and Terminators
	Command-Specific Reference	Perform, Start, Stop
Stop	Exploring Basic Communication	Events, Their Initiators and Terminators
	Command-Specific Reference	Perform, Start, Stop
Structure	Information Communication Examples	Information Reports and Charts
	Command-Specific Reference	Group, Array, Folder, Key, Layout, Shape,

Command	Section	Chapter
		Structure, Template, Theme
Style	Exploring Complex Communication	Do It Again!
	Command-Specific Reference	Define, Condition, Element, Feature, File, Location, Segment, Style, Synonym
Synonym	Exploring Complex Communication	Do It Again!
	Command-Specific Reference	Define, Condition, Element, Feature, File, Location, Segment, Style, Synonym
Template	Information Communication Examples	Information Reports and Charts
	Hi5ive – Aloha Edition Reference	Aloha Edition Commands
	Command-Specific Reference	Group, Array, Folder, Key, Layout, Shape, Structure, Template, Theme
	Summary and Communication Related Examples	Making Reference
Theme	Command-Specific Reference	Group, Array, Folder, Key, Layout, Shape, Structure, Template, Theme

Properties

A property is a value that is assigned to a Command, Routine, Defined-Object, or Group. Property values are defaulted. They're there for you to access and sometimes set.

Everything you specify on an Attribute of a Command is also a Property.

Here is a list of some properties that I mentioned in this book. There are many more. They help you with things that are behind the scenes and some which are not so much behind the scenes.

Alternate-Names
Command
Command-Bracketed-Comment
Command-Bracketed-Comment-is-Displayed
Command-Color
Command-Color-Code
Command-Color-Standard
Command-Description
Command-Emoji
Command-Emoji-Code
Command-Name
Command-Name-Like
Command-Parts
Data-Type
Externally-Available
Hide-Type
Level1, Level2, Level3, etc.
Mask
Object-Type
Options
Parts
Relationships
Show-As
Status
Value
Warning / Error -Already-Issued

Perhaps, I'll expand this list in the next Edition of **Hi5ive.**

The **ShakaBoard** contains the following properties for each Command:

Command-Name
Command-Description
Command-Bracketed-Comment
Command-Bracketed-Comment-is-Displayed
Command-Parts
Command-Emoji
Command-Emoji-Code
Command-Color
Command-Color-Code
Command-Color-Standard
Command-Name-Like

Command-Name is the name of the Command. Like **Define.**

Command-Description is the Description of what the Command does.

Command-Bracketed-Comment is the Bracketed Comment above the Command when it is displayed on the **ShakaBoard.**

Command-Bracketed-Comment-is-Displayed indicates whether the Bracketed Comment is displayed for this Command.

Command-Parts are the parts of the Command.

Command-Emoji is the Emoji for the Command.

Command-Emoji-Code Is the Emoji-Code for the Command.

Command-Color is the Color for the Command.

Command-Color-Code is the Color Code for the Command.

Command-Color-Standard is the standard that named this Command. For Official Website Colors, this is *Website*.

Command-Name-Like specifies that this Command is like a main Command. When **Command-Name** is the same as **Main-Command-Name,** you know that this is a Main Command.

Clarification Words

Clarification Words can be used to keep the Format of a Command Consistent. Sometimes, they can look like they have more meaning. But, they're just there to make parts of a Command optional that usually aren't.

Any, All
None
Nothing, Nowhere
Something, Somewhere

When you see **Something** or **Somewhere,** usually those are being handled by another part of the Command. Those parts are probably being handled by a Routine that's being referenced by that other part of the Command.

Index of Pookay, HakaPookay and HalePookay

This Index contains the name of each **Pookay, HakaPookay,** and **HalePookay** in this book. Each name is followed by a description. Then, it is followed by **Pookay, HakaPookay,** or **HalePookay,** depending on whether it is a Book, a Bookshelf, or a Library.[45] Then, it is followed by each section and chapter where it is found.

The names of all the **Pookay, HakaPookay,** and **HalePookay** in this book are Hawaiian, except **ShakaBoard** and **TalkStory.** If you need help pronouncing them, refer to Appendix B: Hawaiian Pronunciation.

[45] **Book, Bookshelf, Library:** Libraries contain Bookshelves. Bookshelves contain Books.

Ho'ike: Reports: **HakaPookay**
Presentations, Visualizations: Formatting Reports

Kanaka: Person: **Pookay**
Hi5ive – Aloha Edition Reference: Keeping It Clear

Ka'ina: Sort / Sequence: **HakaPookay**
Introduction: More on HakaPookay and HalePookay

Ki'i'Ike: Visual Art (also **2DKi'i'Ike** and **3DKi'i'Ike**): **HakaPookay**
Exploring Complex Communication: Art
Exploring Complex Communication: Do It Again!
Exploring Complex Communication: Dance
Command-Specific Reference: Define, Condition, Element, Feature, File, Location, Segment, Style, Synonym

LeoOLeho: Music: **HakaPookay**
Introduction: Aloha Edition Enhancements
Exploring Complex Communication: Music
Exploring Complex Communication: Dance

Ne'ePeki: Animation (Move Step-by-Step): **HakaPookay**
Exploring Complex Communication: Dance

Pā'aniWikiō: Video Game: **HalePookay**
Presentations, Visualizations: Slideshow / Presentation / Video

Palekana: Security: **HakaPookay**
Information Communication Examples: Information Security

ShakaBoard: Help System: **HalePookay**
Introduction: Aloha Edition Enhancements
Introduction: More on HakaPookay and HalePookay

ShakaBoard (cont.):
Hi5ive – Aloha Edition Reference
Hi5ive – Aloha Edition Reference: ShakaBoard
Hi5ive – Aloha Edition Reference: Emojis and Colors for the Commands
Hi5ive – Aloha Edition Reference: How Will Hi5ive – Aloha Edition Evolve?

TalkStory: Editor for building **Pookay** and **HakaPookay.** Also possibly contains Word Processing routines such as text formatting. Also possibly contains Report, Chart, Dashboard, etc. routines.: **HalePookay**
Introduction: Aloha Edition Enhancements
Introduction: More on HakaPookay and HalePookay
Introduction: Writing Pookay
Presentations, Visualizations: Dashboards and Other Summary Presentations
Hi5ive – Aloha Edition Reference: Command Format

Wikiō: Video Routines: **HakaPookay**
Presentations, Visualizations: Slideshow / Presentation / Video

Appendix A: Definitions of Commonly Used Words

Hi5ive – Original Edition: The first published version of this Language. **Hi5ive – Original Edition** was designed to be the simplest App Building Language.

Hi5ive – Aloha Edition: The second published version of this Language. **Hi5ive – Aloha Edition** expanded, enhance, and clarified **Hi5ive – Original Edition** to make it a simple Language for Communication.

Command: Action. Actually, some of the Commands in **Hi5ive – Aloha Edition** are Definitions or Descriptions, rather than Actions. A Command is a statement that (typically) does something.

We usually think of a Command as a statement that gets somebody else to do something. In App Building Languages, it is the Computer that we are trying to get to do something. In **Hi5ive – Aloha Edition,** the Commands are there to help everyone understand the Communication better.

Routine: A Routine is composed of zero or more Commands. A Routine can be moved away from the main part of an App / **Pookay.** That should help you see the Trees for the Forest.

Routines are generally created when they will be used more than once (probably by multiple Apps / **Pookay**).

Routines are also created when what they do is complex or not straightforward.

When you don't want people to know how a Routine does what it does, place it in a different App / **Pookay.** Your App / **Pookay** will hopefully be able to use that Routine. However, how it does whatever it does, will remain out of your view.

App Building Languages: These are Languages that are used to build Apps. They are also called Computer Programming Languages.

Pookay: A Break-Down of a piece of a Communication. A group of Routines.

HakaPookay: A bookshelf. A collection of **Pookay.** This is vaguely similar to an App.

Object: Something. Some named thing.

Element: A simple, non-complex thing. An elementary, basic thing.

Table: One or more rows and columns. I use Table and File interchangeably, since all Data Tables are actually Files.
Tables exist in a Database. Files that are not Tables do not exist in a Database. However, most App Building Languages can access both. And, some, like either edition of **Hi5ive** do so in the same manner.

Both Files and Tables can be grouped into Folders.

Operator: Mathematical operators include +, -, /, *, =.
Logical operators include and, or, =.

= represent equals as a mathematical operator.

= represents is-equal-to as a logical operator.

If you're reading a print version of this book, feel free to add more definitions here. However, you'll need to paste in more pages.

Appendix B: Hawaiian Pronunciation

First, let me mention that this book contains three languages: English, Hawaiian, and Hawaiian Pidgin. Mostly, it contains English.

With English, there's no telling how a word will be pronounced. I assume you already know how to pronounce most English words. So, I haven't included any help for that.

You can look up Hawaiian pronunciation online. Basically, there are five vowels: a; e; i; o; u. Those are pronounced short a, like ah; long a; long e; long o, and oo.

Consonants are pronounced like they would be in English. Though sometimes, there is some local variation.

The spelling of some Hawaiian words includes the 'okina. The 'okina is represented by a straight single quote '. It is a glottal stop or an almost unspoken g or a very soft fricative breath [a breath pronounced by friction]. Basically, the 'okina keeps two vowels from running together when spoken.

The spelling of some Hawaiian words includes the kahakō (¯). The kahakō is called a macron or an overscore in English. It can appear over any vowel. The kahakō extends the length of the pronunciation of that vowel, but not by much.

'Okina and kahakō are often omitted when Hawaiian words are spelled / written. However, there's a movement to bring them back into writing.

Some words in Hawaiian Pidgin are pronounced like they would be pronounced in English. Some are pronounced like they would be pronounced in Hawaiian. Others, are pronounced however they're pronounced.

In English, a plural of a noun is usually formed by adding an s to the end of the singular word. [Sometimes es is added, rather than just s.] For instance: Dear, Dears.

Yet, there are nouns in English where the plural is the same as the singular. Deer, Deer.

In Hawaiian, the plural form of a noun is the same as the singular. However, the Hawaiian word for *the* usually precedes that noun. The singular form of *the* is *ke* or *ka*. The plural form is nā. Other methods for making plurals in Hawaiian are found at Wikipedia.[46]

I omit ke / ka when using Hawaiian words in **Hi5ive – Aloha Edition.** I also don't try to distinguish between the singular and plural form of that word. You'll need to gather whether a Hawaiian word is singular or plural from context. Not that!

[46] **Hawaiian Plurals:** https://en.wikipedia.org/wiki/Hawaiian_grammar

Appendix C: Other Communication Frameworks

I use **Hi5ive – Aloha Edition** to help me break down pieces of a Communication so that everybody can understand them in the same way. I refer to those pieces of Communication as Frameworks.

They might be Communication Frameworks as far as App Building is concerned. However, they're not what is typically thought of as a Communication Framework.

I've listed the first Communication Frameworks that I found on the Internet below, for you to reference. Most of them just list the order in which to place things in a Communication.

The Communication Frameworks that I would use with **Hi5ive – Aloha Edition** are different. I would call them *Flow* or *Desired Flow* or perhaps *Break-Down* or *Essential Bits.* I might call them *Points to Agree On.*

I suppose that you could use **Hi5ive – Aloha Edition** with any of those Communication Frameworks or to help you create any of those Frameworks.[47] If that's helpful, go for it!

Please let me know if you do that. I'm curious about how that would work.

---

[47] **Please do not use Hi5ive – Aloha Edition with The Enemy Framework.** I do not see stressing that something is the enemy as a positive, helpful way to Communicate.

Also, please don't use it with **Nit**. Please, don't do as this Communication Framework suggests and just point out when you're nitpicking. Just please don't nitpick. Nobody appreciates it. And, it's not helpful.

In the list of Communication Frameworks, I've marked some with that I don't think are helpful.

Noah Kennedy tells us about four Communication Frameworks on Medium.[48] I summarize those as:

- **BLUF** stands for *Bottom Line Up Front*. Place the *bottom line* at the beginning. Details follow the bottom line.
- **Business Chemistry** [coined by Deloitte]. Speak to your Audience.
- **I Intend.** State what you intend to do before you say how you're going to do it.
- **Nit.** Precede Nitpicking with *Nit.*

Falk Rehkopf lists seven Communication Frameworks on his Blog.[49] His list includes **BLUF.** The rest are listed below:

- **What? So What? Now What?**
- **REE.** Recommendation, Evaluation, Expectation.
- **Think, Feel, Do.**[50]
- **CBIN** (for delivering feedback). Context, Behavior, Impact, Next Steps.
- **The Enemy Framework.**
- **Name, Same, Fame, Aim, Game.**

All of those names, except **The Enemy Framework,** tell you the order in which to present your Communication. **The**

---

[48] **Noah Kennedy on Medium: Four Communication Frameworks:** https://noahlk.medium.com/key-communication-frameworks-for-individual-contributors-e18142a2c66f

[49] **Falk Rehkopf on his Blog: Seven Communication Frameworks:** https://www.falkrehkopf.com/blog/7-must-know-communication-frameworks-for-leaders

[50] Rob Biesenbach on his Blog calls this Know, Feel, Do. **https://robbiesenbach.com/a-simple-communication-framework-for-crafting-any-message/**

Enemy Framework tells a story about an enemy. This is who the enemy is. This is what will happen if we do nothing about the enemy. This is what we're going to do to defeat that enemy. **The Enemy Framework** is **What? So What? Now What?** where *What* is The Enemy.

Preston Chin's Blog lists three Communications Frameworks.[51] These include **What? So What? Now What?**

- **PREP:** Point, Reason, Example, Point. State your point at both the beginning and at the end.
- **TOP-T:** Topic, Orient, Point, Transition. This can be used for Slideshow Presentations. Orient means to explain what each slide is talking about. Transition refers to the transitions between slides. I would use Segue instead of Transition. But, then, the abbreviation would be TOP-S.

[51] **Preston Chin's Blog: Communication Frameworks:** https://www.prestonchin.co/blog/3-frameworks-to-talk-smart-on-the-spot

Appendix D: Where to Find Emojis and Colors

As you add Commands, you should add an Emoji to identify it by. The Color will be the same as the Command that you base your Command on. If your new Command is not based on another Command, you'll want to give it a Color. You can find more Emojis at:

- My Unicode Website[52]
- Emojipedia.com
- Amp-what.com
- Compart's Unicode Website[53]
- FileFormat.info

These websites tell you the code to copy-and-paste. My Website, Emojipedia, and Amp-what also allow you to copy the Emoji itself.

Note: Some of the codes on Amp-what don't always show completely and/or they're in a different format. **Bottom-line:** If you need that code, try to find the same symbol on one of the other websites.

Technically, you can use any Unicode Symbol for the Emoji. Unicode Symbols include letters, numbers, punctuation, accented characters, Emojis, non-English Characters, and more.

Emojipedia only shows you Emojis, rather than the more complete set of Unicode Symbols.

The other References that I've shared show you the majority of the Unicode Symbols.

---

[52] **My Unicode Website:** https://stubbart.com/computer_consulting/unicode/index.html

[53] **Compart's Unicode Website:** https://www.compart.com/en/unicode

Try not to use any Unicode Symbol that look like a tall rectangle. There are several of those. The Tall Rectangle means that that Unicode Symbol does not display correctly.

Also, don't try to use any Country or State Flag. Windows displays the two-character code for that Country or State instead.

For the Colors and their Codes, refer to my website of the Official Colors for Websites.[54] You are not limited to the Official Website Colors.

If you use a Non-Official Color, you'll have to figure out an appropriate name for the **ShakaBoard** and **TalkStory.**

To find Colors and their Codes, I would first suggest that you look at my website which shows more *Official Colors* from multiple sources, not just the Official Colors for Websites.[55]

Emojis and Colors for Various Commands

The **Emoji & Code** column below contains the Emoji, its description, and its technical code.

You can Copy the Emoji Symbol to **ShakaBoard.**Command-Emoji. **ShakaBoard.**Command-Emoji-Code will automatically be filled in.

You can Copy the Emoji Code to **ShakaBoard.**Command-Emoji-Code. And,

[54] **My Website of the Official Colors for Websites:** https://stubbart.com/computer_consulting/color_themes/color_closest.html

[55] **More Official Colors:** https://stubbart.com/computer_consulting/color_themes/color_all.html

ShakaBoard. Command-Emoji will automatically be filled in.[56]

ShakaBoard. Command-Color contains the Color Name. **ShakaBoard.**Command-Color-Code contains the Color Code.[57] If you Copy a Color Name to **ShakaBoard.**Command-Color and it's an Official Website Color, **ShakaBoard.**Command-Color-Code will contain the Color Code automatically.

ShakaBoard. Command-Color-Code-Standard will default to Website, if **ShakaBoard.**Command-Color is an Official Website Color. Override this, if the Color is from some other Standard.

Command	Emoji & Code	Color & Code
Command	⩩ Grid ⩩	Black #000000
Comment	㸚 x x x x 㸚	Light Gray #AFAFAF
Copy	⟷ Long Left-Right Arrow ⟷	Medium Green #006600
Copy => Draw	🖌️ Paintbrush 🖌️	**Copy** Color
Copy => MoveFrom	⊗ Circled X ⊗	**Copy** Color
Copy => Reset	🙅🏽 Person saying No 🙅🏽	**Copy** Color
Copy => Set	🙆🏽 Person saying OK 🙆🏽	**Copy** Color

[56] **Emoji Codes:** I use the Hexadecimal format of the code value. You can use the Decimal format if you're more comfortable with that.

[57] **Color Codes:** I use the Hexadecimal format of the Color Code. You can use any valid CSS format of the Color Code: RGB, RGBA, HSL, and more. https://developer.mozilla.org/en-US/docs/Web/CSS/color_value

Hi5ive – Aloha Edition

A Simple Language for
Communicating with Deep Understanding

Command	Emoji & Code	Color & Code
Define	🛠️ Hammer and Wrench 🛠️	Medium Blue #0000BF
Define => Condition	⍰ Enclosed Question Mark [? Question Mark=**If**] ⍰	**Define** Color
Define => Element	⊙ Dot in Circle (Hydrogen – 1st Element) ⊙	**Define** Color
Define => Feature	🖌️ Paintbrush 🖌️	**Define** Color
Define => File	🗐 Multiple Pages 🗐	**Define** Color
Define => Location	⚓ Anchor ⚓	**Define** Color
Define => Segment	🠶 Lines and Arcs 🠶	**Define** Color
Define => Style	ξ Greek Letter xi ξ	**Define** Color
Define => Synonym	≛ Star Equals ≛	**Define** Color
Group	🉁 Grouped Lines 🉁	Light Blue #0000FF
Group => Array	≣ 4 horizontal lines ≣	**Group** Color
Group => Folder	📂 Open File Folder 📂	**Group** Color
Group => Key	🔑 Key 🔑	**Group** Color

Hi5ive – Aloha Edition

A Simple Language for
Communicating with Deep Understanding

Command	Emoji & Code	Color & Code
Group => Layout	📰 Open newspaper 📰	**Group** Color
Group => Shape	💠 Dot within Diamond 💠	**Group** Color
Group => Structure	🔡 a b c d 🔡	**Group** Color
Group => Template	⧆ Asterisk inside Square ⧆	**Group** Color
Group => Theme	🎨 Artist's Pallet 🎨	**Group** Color
If	？ Full-Width Question Mark ？	Medium Purple #6F307F
Perform	⟲ Circle Arrow ⟲	Light Green #00BF00
Perform => Start	↦ Rightwards Arrow from Bar ↦	**Perform** Color
Perform => Stop	⇥ Rightwards Arrow to Bar ⇥	**Perform** Color
Person	🧑🏽 Person 🧑🏽	Tan #7F7F00
Person => Role	🥸 Disguised Face 🥸	**Person** Color
Routine	ㅇ Circle ㅇ	Dark Gray #7F7F7F
Security	🔒 Lock 🔒	Dark Red #8B0000

Appendix E: Hi5ive – Aloha Edition Comparison

This Appendix shows the differences between **Hi5ive - Aloha Edition** and some App Building Languages.

This Appendix is primarily for those who are familiar with App Building Languages. Still, feel free to read it even if you aren't familiar with App Building Languages. You might need to know those things if you get deeply involved with **Hi5ive - Aloha Edition.** I tried to keep things simple.

Uppercase [Capital Letters] / Lowercase [No Capital Letters] / Mixed Case [Both Uppercase and Lowercase Letters]

Hi5ive - Aloha Edition keeps the Command appearance consistent without making it rigid. For instance, Commands and Keywords in **Hi5ive - Aloha Edition** are not case sensitive. You can say **Define, define, DEFINE,** or **DeFINE.** In fact, only text literals, like "Abc" [or Abc] are case sensitive. This means that "Abc" is different from "abc" and therefore not equal to it.

In some App Building Languages, case is super important. When, it is, **Define, define, DEFINE,** or **DeFINE** are all different.

Ways to End a Command

See Ways to End a Command below in the chapter If Command Differences.

Comments

Most App Building Languages do not have a **Comment** Command.[58] Many just offset comments with some sort of punctuation like /* Comment */.

To make the syntax of each Edition of **Hi5ive** consistent, even with Comments, I created the **Comment** Command.

Elements

Elements are called variables in most other App Building Languages.[59] However, an Element can be less limiting than just variables. And, Element is some basic thing. As such, an Element can be something that isn't a variable. A Variable is something that is likely to vary / change.

This

Some App Building Languages allow you to use the keyword This.[60] In **Hi5ive - Aloha Edition,** I could have provided This.

Routine.This would have referred to the current routine
Array.This would have referred to the Array of the current **Group** Command.

---

[58] **Comments in various Languages:** https://en.wikipedia.org/wiki/Comparison_of_programming_Languages_(syntax)#Comments

[59] **IBM's take on what variables are referred to in COBOL:** https://www.ibm.com/docs/en/cobol-zos/6.3.0?topic=data-using-variables-structures-literals-constants

[60] **this in Javascript.** https://www.w3schools.com/js/js_this.asp this is lowercase in Javascript. This is used similarly in some other App Building Languages.

If I had provided **This,** I would have called it **Current.**

However, I didn't provide **This** because I find it to be confusing.[61] It takes me a while to figure out what **This** is referring to because it can refer to different things based on various factors.

I also didn't provide This in **Hi5ive - Aloha Edition** because it can cause issues when you modify a **Pookay.** What if you, later on, split a Routine of a **Pookay** in two? Does This now represent what you think it represents?

Using Quotes

A, B, and C can be the names of Elements. Elements hold text or numbers. Text and Numbers can be specified as they are, like Hi and 5.

In most App Building Languages, text needs to be surrounded by quotes (single quotes or double quotes or either, depending on that Language).

Surrounding text with quotes is optional in **Hi5ive - Aloha Edition.** Use them when you need to make things clearer. Use curly quotes, since a straight quote is used as the 'okina (glottal stop) in some Hawaiian words.

[61] **This can be confusing.** While This can be a useful shortcut, it can also be confusing. I don't use this in Javascript, where it is available. And, I write quite a bit of Javascript.

Definition-Scope

In both editions of **Hi5ive,** when something is defined[62] in a Routine, it is only available within that Routine. In other App Building Languages, we would say that it is local to that Routine. In other words, it has a local scope. It is unknown outside of that Routine.

When something is defined in an App outside of all Routines, it is available everywhere within that App, including in those Routines. In other App Building Languages, we would say that it has a global scope.

Some App Building Languages allow further localization when defining something. For instance something can be defined as only being available within a **Perform.**[63] In other App Building Languages, we would say that it has a block scope.

In **Hi5ive - Aloha Edition,** things can be defined within a **Pookay** / **HakaPookay** / **HalePookay** or within a Routine. Yet, even those things that are defined within a Routine are accessible outside of that Routine unless their **Externally-Available** Property is **False.**

Externally-Available can also be **True** or the names of Routines, etc. where it is available.

Some other App Building Languages let you Define Elements (text, numbers, dates) by just mentioning the name of a Defined-Object. Some App Building Languages know the **Data-Type** of

[62] [Something can be **defined** using **Define** and Commands like **Define.** Something can also be defined using **Group** and Commands like **Group.**]

[63] Command that are equivalent to **Perform** in other languages include **For** and **While.**

those Defined Objects because that is implied by the first letter of the Object-Name.

That has always been as clear as mud to me. And, it's one further thing to memorize. So, I often define Elements in those Languages even though I don't have to.

In **Hi5ive,** everything is Defined. We do that because we're striving for clear Communication.

Hi5ive - Aloha Edition has something else that helps with scope. It's called Command Level.

```
Perform.Level1 ...
    ...
    Perform.Level2 ...
    End-Perform.Level2
End-Perform.Level1
```

I've often wished that **HTML** provided something like that. My websites have so many nested **<div>'s** that it's almost impossible to line them up. I'm sure other's websites are the same.

I came up with a solution that allows me to use **<level1>...</level1>**, **<level2>...</level2>** etc. instead.[64] You can also give each **<div>** an ID and include that in a comment after the **</div>.**

---

[64] **<level1> ...:** See my x_press functions for Expressive Websites at https://stubbart.com/computer_consulting/code/index.html

Math and Logical Operators

Hi5ive - Aloha Edition uses +, -, *, / for plus, minus, times, and divide. That's standard for Math and for App Building Languages.

Several App Building Languages use **&&** for **and**. They also use **||** for **or. Hi5ive - Aloha Edition** uses **and** and **or.**

Hi5ive - Aloha Edition uses the standard <, > for is-less-than, is-greater-than. = is used for both equals and is-equal-to. Most App Building Languages use <= for is-less-than-or-equal-to and >= for is greater-than-or-equal-to. Notice that = always comes last. The **Aloha Edition** doesn't care whether = comes first or last.

Connecting Things Together

Concatenate means to link things together. In App Building Languages, it means to string things together or to connect them together, one after the other.

If I concatenate **black** and **cat,** I get **blackcat.** I probably wanted **black cat.** So, I can concatenate **"black "** and **"cat".** Or, I can concatenate **black, 1space,** and **cat.**

Some App Building Languages use + as the concatenation operator.[65]

Some use &.[66]

Some use ||.[67]

Most App Building Languages also have a **Concat** or a **Concatenate** Routine.

[65] **Javascript** uses + as the concatenation operator.
[66] **Excel** uses & as the concatenation operator.
[67] **SQL** uses || as the concatenation operator.

Hi5ive - Aloha Edition

A Simple Language for
Communicating with Deep Understanding

Hi5ive - Aloha Edition provides the **Connect** Routine. The Parameters for this routine are How you want to connect the parts, the Result, and the parts that you want to connect.

How you want to connect the parts is the **Connect-Type.** It can be simple like **1space**, **1period**, **1slash**, or **Nothing.** It can be more complex. If it gets very complex, create your own Routine.

Hi5ive - Aloha Edition also provides **Template.** This Command is used to connect parts.

Spaces around Operators

App Building Languages might look at all of the Defined-Objects and see if **Phone-Work** is defined as one object or two (**Phone** minus **Work**).

Sometimes App Building Languages do not allow a hyphen in object names. Those that don't often allow an underscore instead. Though, there are some App Building Languages that allow both.

Some App Building Languages, including **Hi5ive** assume that the dash is a minus only when it is surrounded by spaces as in **Phone - Work.**

Number of =

Some App Building Languages distinguish between =, ==, and ===. In simple terms, those represent equal, more equal, and most equal.

Hi5ive - Aloha Edition doesn't make that distinction. It just uses =. If it does need to make that distinction, use a qualification that specifies how something is more or most equal. For instance, if you're imitating most of those languages that use == and ===, use **logically-equal** and **(value-equal and data-type-equal).**

If and End-If Differences

There are no great synonyms for **If.** There's **Provided-That,** which I sometimes use. Still, I find **If** to be less clunky most of the time.

Instead of **If,** I could have called this Command **Decide** because **If** is making a Decision.

Ways to end a Command.

In particular, the **If** Command:

- Some App Building Languages[68] end **If** and other Commands by ending the line.
- Some use a period.[69]
- Some end **If** with **End If.** Some use **End_If**. Some use **EndIf**. And, some use **End-If.**[70] [Those periods are merely punctuation to keep the grammar straight in this book. They are not needed in those App Building Languages.] Many of those languages do not provide **End ...** for most of the Commands.
- Some App Building Languages enclose other parts of **If** (besides the Condition) in **{}**. In some of those Languages, if you don't use **{}**, only the first Command following the Condition is part of the **If** or **Else.**[71]

---

[68] **Some Early Versions of RPG ended If by ending the line.** Python might be included here. However, it's really relying on ending the indentation.

[69] **COBOL can end an If or any Command with a period.** Modern **COBOL** can use **END-IF** instead.

[70] **Variations on End-If:**
https://en.wikipedia.org/wiki/Comparison_of_programming_languages_(syntax)
Note: End_If is not listed. You can search for that separately and find a few examples.

[71] **C, Java, Javascript, Python and more.**
https://en.wikipedia.org/wiki/List_of_programming_languages_by_type#Curly_bracket_languages

- At least one App Building Language reverses the Command. So, **If** is ended by **Fi.**[72] [**Eef** is ended by **Fee. Of** is ended by **Fo.** And, **Muf** is ended by **Fum.** Just kidding.]
- One App Building Language uses indentation to end **If.**[73] When a Command starts at the same position as the preceding **If**, the line before it ends the Then portion or the Else portion of the **If**.

In **Hi5ive – Aloha Edition,** you can use **EndIf, End If, End-If,** or **End_If. End_If** requires you to press the shift key to create the **_**. And, that can break the rhythm of your typing.

Other Parts of If

Usually, when speaking, Then is omitted from an **If** sentence. The main reason for Then is to indicate the end of the Condition (Today=Friday). Some App Building Languages place the Condition within () and don't need a Then. We might say Next or In that Case, rather than Then.

Also, since there can be an Else, Then helps things stay consistent. This makes it easier to quickly see the big picture.

I don't use Else much when I'm writing books. I don't see it being used in other people's books. I almost never hear it in conversation. So, perhaps, there's a better word.

Some App Building Languages use Otherwise in place of Else. Otherwise is often limited to situations where there are more than two options, not just one Then and one Else.

If not is another option for Else. But, that can easily become confused with **If.**

---

[72] **Fi ends If in Unix Bash, sh, and ksh shell languages.** https://en.wikipedia.org/wiki/Comparison_of_programming_languages_(syntax)

[73] **Python uses indentation (or rather indentation alignment) to end If.** I like Python. But, using indentation to detect the end of a Command? Really?!!

The best alternative for **Else** might be **For all other Conditions** or **When all else fails**.

A simpler alternative for **Else** might be **Also** or **ThenAlso.**

Rather than trying to replace each word individually, we can use a less direct approach.

Consider this example:

```
If Today=Friday
  When True I eat pizza
  When False I eat a sandwich
End-If
```

We can also say it this way:

```
If Today=Friday
  Then I eat pizza
End-If
If Today not= Friday
  Then I eat a sandwich
End-If
```

We can also say:

```
X=sandwich
If Today=Friday
  Then X=pizza
End-If
Y=I eat x
```

Some App Building Languages provide a **Case** Command. Some versions of **Case** are useful when you need to check several different conditions. If this version of **Case** were provided, it would have several **Then**s. Some App Building Languages only provide **Case,** rather than both **If** and **Case.** Some App Building Languages call **Case** ***Switch.***

Some App Building Languages provide a Function / Routine that acts like an **If** Command. Some of these Functions are called:

- IF[74]
- IFF[75]
- IIF[76]
- Coalesce[77]

---

[74] **The IF Function** is available in **Excel** and in the **Google Docs Editor.**

[75] **The IFF Function** is mostly used in various versions of **SQL.**

[76] **The IIF Function** is available in **Access** and **SQL Server SQL.**

[77] **The Coalesce Function** is available in various versions of **SQL.** Coalesce can check several conditions, just like Case.

File-Types

Common **File-Types** include .txt (text), .html (HTML website), .js (javascript), .css (Cascading Style Sheet), .docx (Word document), .xlsx (Excel Spreadsheet), etc. As you can see many Common **File-Types** are four characters are less in length. Still, not all **File-Types** are that short.

In **Hi5ive - Aloha Edition,** we have **File-Types** of **Pookay, HakaPookay, HalePookay,** and others. Plus, we might want to prefix those that are unique to **Hi5ive - Aloha Edition** with **Hi5ive - Aloha Edition.** That will make those **File-Types** very long. That might make them longer than the file name.

That doesn't really matter. In Windows, the length of the filename plus the length of the **File-Type** (extension) cannot exceed 255 characters. That should be plenty long enough.

However, for visual considerations, we can make those file-types shorter.

The easiest way to do that is to remove some of the vowels. For instance, we could use **Hi5A-Pky** for **Pookay. Hi5A-HkPky** is a little long. But, I think it will do.

If we need to make them shorter, we can use numbers. **Hi5A-HkPky** could be **Hi5A2** for the second **File-Type** that is unique to **Hi5ive - Aloha Edition.** [At this point, who knows if Pookay is the second **File-Type** that is unique to **Hi5ive - Aloha Edition.** This is just an example.]

Classes, Data-Types, Object-Types, Methods

Some App Building Languages provide the **Class** Command.[78] **Class** allows App Builders to create Data-Types that aren't built into that App Building Language.

That might come in handy at some point. But, for now, you can assume that any Data-Type or Object-Type you could ever want to use is built into **Hi5ive – Aloha Edition.** And, if it isn't, you can define it with **Define.**

If the name of the Data-Type or Object-Type does not make it immediately clear what that Data-Type or Object-Type is, you can add a Comment.

If you find yourself missing, wanting, or needing the **Class** Command, you can add it.

I mainly mention the **Class** Command because some examples of some App Building Languages make it seem like it's always required, even though it might not be.

COBOL is on the list of Class-Based App Building Languages in that reference note at the top of this chapter. I've programmed in **COBOL** like forever and I never knew that until today.

It appears to me that **Class** was added so that **Java** could interact with **COBOL** (or vice-versa). So, maybe **Class** will need

[78] **The Class Command** can be used in **Typescript, C++, Java, Ruby,** and more App Building Languages. https://en.wikipedia.org/wiki/Category:Class-based_programming_languages, However, in some of those, Class isn't a Command, even though it provides the same functionality.

to be added to **Hi5ive - Aloha Edition** so that it can interact with some App Building Languages.

Apparently **Java** and **Smalltalk** require Classes. In most other App Building Languages, when **Class** is available, it's optional. So, if you're accessing an App that's written in **Java** or **Smalltalk,** you'll probably need to add the **Class** Command to **Hi5ive - Aloha Edition.**

If it were me, I would try to find a similar routine that was written in a different App Building Language and use that. I might even try to rewrite that logic from scratch in **Hi5ive - Aloha Edition.**

You can already reference a Class that's used in some Routine that's written in some App Building Language. Just say **App-Name.Routine-Name.Class-Name.**

App Building Languages might want to access Classes in **Hi5ive - Aloha Edition.** They won't have much luck since Classes don't exist there. If they insist, I might have to add **Class** to **Hi5ive - Aloha Edition.** But, perhaps, I'll call it something else more meaningful like **UserDefinition** or **User-Defined-Type.**

Along with Classes, **Java**, and some other App Building Languages use Methods. Methods are simply Routines.

Alternate Names for Names within Hi5ive – Aloha Edition

There are no restrictions on Names within **Hi5ive - Aloha Edition.** They can contain Letter of the English Alphabet, Letters of other Alphabets, Numbers, Special Symbols, Emojis, etc.

[Since some Emojis are associated with Commands, you might not want to use Emojis in your **Aloha Edition** Names. Still, there's no restriction that says you can't.]

Names within App Building Languages are often required to be made up solely of Letters of the English Alphabet and Numbers. Often they have to start with a Letter. But, what if you want to reference something in **Hi5ive - Aloha Edition,** that doesn't use those restrictions, from an App that does?

In addition to their given names, any name within the **Aloha Edition, HakaPookay / HalePookay** that the **Aloha Edition** is aware of, and any name within a **Pookay** / Routine that you've written, also has multiple Alternate Names.

The first set of Alternate Names is provided for App Building Languages that require all names to be totally UPPERCASE or lowercase:

So, FirstName becomes:

- FIRSTNAME
- firstname

These Alternate Names are stored in FirstName.AlternateNames. They are stored there automatically.

<==>

Some App Builders prefer that the first letter is always lowercase.

So, **FirstName** becomes:

- **firstName**

<==>

Alternate Names for Hawaiian Names that contain the 'okina and/or kahakō are supplied as follows:

- Vowels that are combined with the kahakō, are replaced with the letter without that diacritical mark. So, ō is replaced with o, ā is replaced with a, etc.
- 'Okina (') are replaced with g. g is not a letter in the Hawaiian Alphabet. And, the 'okina is a guttural stop. So, g for *guttural*. Another alternate name simply removes the 'okina.

So **Pā'aniWikiō** has Alternate Names of:

- **PaaniWikio**
- **PaganiWikio**

<==>

All names that are defined in **Hi5ive - Aloha Edition** that include hyphens and/or underscores have the following alternate names:

- Hyphens become underscores
- Underscores become hyphens
- Both hyphens and underscores are removed.

So **Command-Name** has Alternate Names of:

- **Command_Name**
- **CommandName**

<==>

If a name contains a special symbol (not a Letter or a Number), that symbol is spelled out. That special symbol is also abbreviated when the name of that special symbol is longer than the abbreviation.

So, **Half!Pound** has Alternate Names of:

- **HalfexclamationPound**
- **HalfexclPound**

😁Days has Alternate Names of:

- BeamingFaceWithSmilingEyesDays
- BeamingFaceDays
- BeamingDays
- BeamDays
- 1F601Days [1F601 is the code for that Emoji.]

<==>

If a name starts with a Number, that Number is spelled out and then followed by that Number. Another Aternate Name is made by placing an n before the leading Number to indicate Number.

So, **1DollarBill** has Alternate Names of:

- **One1DollarBill**
- **n1DollarBill**

Note: In this and other cases, more Alternate Names are supplied that follow the UPPERCASE / lowercase and other rules that apply.

This seems like an inordinately large number of Alternate Names when you consider everything that would have Alternate Names. So, perhaps, they're only generated when they're accessed by an App Building Language when and as needed.

What Time Is It?

Often, Timing Commands in an App Building Language are based on the time of the local computer. Sometimes, they're based on the time of a main computer.

Different computers can have different current times at the same time. That usually happens when the time on a Computer needs to be reset – perhaps during a restart.

Usually, that difference between various times is small enough that it doesn't matter. When it does matter, computers should retrieve the current time from the atomic clock every so often. They should especially do that when the time is reset.[79]

That should theoretically happen. However, it doesn't always happen for various reasons.

That possible time difference does not warrant any changes to **Hi5ive - Aloha Edition.** If you need to worry about it, create your own **Pookay.** You can let your **Pookay** reset the Time on all your computers to the time on the Atomic Clock.

Of course, if your **Pookay** can't access an atomic clock [internet is down], you'll want to revert back to using the time of a local computer until the atomic clock becomes available again.

[79] **Atomic Clock:** https://en.wikipedia.org/wiki/Atomic_clock

Going Somewhere?

Generally speaking, in an App, one Command happens, then the next, then the next, then the next, then the next, all the way to the end of the App. This is called *Top-Down Structured* or *Top-Down-Structured Flow*.

However, Routines are generally not part of that flow. Routines are all placed at the bottom of an App in **Hi5ive – Aloha Edition.** When the first Routine Command is encountered, the App stops. Other App Building Languages might handle the flow differently. They might need to know about the Routine before they perform it.

In **Hi5ive – Aloha Edition,** Routines happen when they are referenced. Often, that reference is part of a **Perform** Command.

Going from the top to the bottom of an App is all very well and good for an App Building Language, most of the time. Yet, Communication is not always that regulated. Sometimes, we want to revisit a topic more deeply. Sometimes, we want to skip ahead.

Most App Building Languages provide a mechanism to skip around. Sometimes, they provide multiple means.

Continue, **Break**, and **Exit** or similar Commands might be provided.

Continue does nothing. It's added for clarity. **Continue** means, just keep trucking!

Break ends a Command or a Routine.

Exit can end a Routine. Or, it can go to some other Command. Sometimes, **Exit** is named **Go** or **Go To.**

In App Building Languages, Labels can be attached to Commands.

Example:

Label.Command

Labels are specified as part of **Exit, Go,** or **Go To** Commands. When that Command happens, the App goes to that Label.

Command Labels are also called Tags. In **Hi5ive - Aloha Edition,** they are called App Destinations.

Go (by any name) used to be used a lot in App Building Languages. Sometimes **Go** was used so much that no **Perform** was ever used. This could make an App run very quickly. It could also make that App nearly impossible to maintain. So, Top-Down Flow[80] was introduced.

In **Hi5ive - Aloha Edition,** if you want to stop a Command or a Routine, you can use the **Stop** Command. When you stop a Command, the next Command that happens is the next Command after the current **End-***Command.* When you stop a Routine, the next Command that happens is the End-Perform of the **Perform** Command that started that Routine. In other words, Looping is evaluated to see whether that Routine is performed again or not.

Stop If
End-Stop

Stop Routine-Get-Account-Information

[80] **Top-Down Flow:** https://en.wikipedia.org/wiki/Bottom-up_and_top-down_approaches

End-Stop

What if you want to skip around in the App? What if you want to go to a particular command in the App? Then, you use the **Start** Command.

I strongly recommended that you don't do this. It can make the App very difficult to maintain. Still, if you are going to do this, follow the instructions below.

First you use the **Define** Command to define an App Destination.

Define Destination-A
  As App-Destination
End-Define

Then you use **Start** to go to that App Destination.

Start **Pookay-C.**Destination-A
End-Start

Or

Start Routine-B.Destination-A
End-Start

You can omit Routine-B when the current Command is within Routine-B. Likewise, if you're in the main part of a **Pookay,** rather than in a Routine, you don't need to specify that **Pookay.**

In the above example, **Define** defines that Destination as being at the **Define** command. If you want to define it somewhere else, use the Options attribute. The following defines Destination-A as being the first **If** in Routine-A.

```
Define Destination-A-If
  As App-Destination
  Options At=Routine-A.Command(If)
End-Define
```

In Communication, we tend to label a part of the Communication at the point in time when we want to talk about it.

Do you remember when we were talking about such-and-so?

"*Such-and-so*" is a Communication-Destination.

In an App, we generally need to know where we might want to go a long time before the App goes there. We generally need to know it when we write the App.

Dynamically labeling a place within an App is extremely difficult. **Hi5ive - Aloha Edition** theoretically allows for this in the **Define** syntax. See the previous **Define** example.

App Editors

Hi5ive - Aloha Edition uses the **TalkStory** as its Communications Editor.

- Many Microsoft App Languages (**Visual Basic, Visual C, C++,** etc.) use the **Microsoft Visual Studio Editor** to edit Apps.
- **Jupyter Notebook, Microsoft Visual Studio Editor, PyCharm** and other Editors can be used with **Python.**
- For website programming and Python, I use **Notepad++.**
- For **COBOL,** I usually use **UltraEdit.**

There are many more App Editors. Most of those I have not used or heard of.

Depending on the App Building Language you might not have a choice of Editors.

You might also be limited to the Editor that's installed on your Computer or Computer Network. That's because some Companies prefer one Editor over another.

You can use any Editor with **Hi5ive - Aloha Edition,** provided that Editor allows you to use **Hi5ive - Aloha Edition** with it. Still, you'll need to treat what you've written in **Hi5ive - Aloha Edition** as a text file. That's because no Editor is aware of **Hi5ive - Aloha Edition** yet.

TalkStory is a much nicer Editor for **Hi5ive - Aloha Edition.** It creates the Command for you. Then, you can change what you need to change. But, since **TalkStory** doesn't yet exist, you'll need to use a different Editor. Some Editor's allow you to add a new Language and rules for formatting and perhaps syntax-checking that language. If you figure out how to make that work for **Hi5ive - Aloha Edition,** please let me know.

One of the nicest things about Editors is that most of them can align a Command and parts of a Command for you. I didn't have that luxury when writing this book. Aligning Commands and parts of Command in **Microsoft Word** was not an easy feat.

If you're writing **Hi5ive - Aloha Edition** on a WhiteBoard or by hand, you might wish to keep as much of a Command on one-line as possible in order to save space.

Bolding might be hard to achieve by hand.
I suggest drawing an outlined first character of the Command. E.g. Command ... End-Command.
Another way to simulate bolding, is to precede or surround the Command with =>, <= or some other special character(s). E.g. =>Command<= ... =>End-Command<=.

I used **Microsoft Word** to write this book and all of the **Hi5ive - Aloha Edition** Examples. In those Examples I used the following fonts:

- **Hi5ive (both Editions) and similar things like App Building Language Names, Routine-Names, etc.:** DejaVu Sans **Bold.**
- **Commands:** Congenial. Command Name is **Bold.** End-Command is **Bold.** Attributes are Underlined.
- **0-9+=*/#$<> and perhaps other special characters:** Consolas.

www.ingramcontent.com/pod-product-compliance
Lightning Source LLC
LaVergne TN
LVHW090314210926
848480LV00001B/243
* 9 7 9 8 2 3 2 1 4 7 1 0 5 *